Saturday night girl

CHRISTOPHER KYPREOS

RUNNING MAN EDITIONS
London

First published in 2010
by Running Man Editions
5 Leopold Road London NW10 9LN
UK

www.christopherkypreos.com
email: rmeditions@yahoo.com

Editorial +44 (0) 20 8453 0148
Distribution +44 (0) 79 0644 7201

A CIP Record for this book
is available from the British Library

ISBN 978-0-900793-03-5

Contents

I
Singing for paperclips

II
Saturday night girl

III
A moment out of time

I

Singing for paperclips

For Christine and Sophie

Sappho's mother 16.15.39

Come to mama, come to mama, do…

When I refused,
you waived a trinket
or some other object of desire
to lure me to your side.
But when I claimed it
you snatched it
from my grasping fingers
with a crafty regard...
And with that empty-
handed look
I was corrupted.

Yesterday,
I happened on these
lines of Sappho's:
When I was little
I knew better than
to turn down some
bauble or other
my mother would
hold out to me
- or words to that effect.

Amazing. Same experience.
Same Greek mother.
Twenty-six-hundred
years before.

Boogieman 07.02.39

We left the house to take
a walk in Prospect Park.
It was a sunny afternoon.
Pointing at a thin black man
who lived next door
my mother said,
This is the Boogieman.
If you don't watch your step,
he'll be coming after you.

I searched his face for
some sign of evil intent
but I could find none:
a gaunt man in his seventies,
over-dressed in worn-
out corduroy and tweed
- too warm for summer -
standing in a doorway
lost in thought
gazing up at the rooftops
on Simpson Street in the Bronx
at two in the afternoon
just before the outbreak
of the Second World War.

As we passed him
I took note of his appearance
so that I would recognise him
if we met again.
The Boogieman.

Mr mellowroll 07.13.39

Popping heart pills out of
a pimpled plastic sheet, today,
I connected with 1939.
That day I craved a paper
strip of sugar dots
from the candy-store
across the street.
But the shop was closed.
My mother said it was
a Jewish holiday
and that it wouldn't
open again
until morning.

I craved the sweetness
right then (and still do).
She tried to mollify
my anger,
though I could
only think about
my sugar fix.
How dare he close
the candy store,
leaving me seething
with rage because
of some dumb holiday?

It is true that
in the unconscious
there is no yesterday!

03.13.03

Vases 08.08.39

She was lying on the floor,
listening to the radio.
It was a big freestanding
contraption that whistled
and squawked when you
tuned-in a station.
He walked into the room
and switched it off.
She said, *Hey ,I was listening to that!*
He said, *No, you weren't.*
You were asleep.
She insisted she wasn't.
He argued otherwise.

This soon escalated into
a full-blown battle,
with vases flying back
and forth across the room.
All because my brother was jealous
and controlling of his space.
He couldn't let my sister
play the radio while she slept,
not in *that* house,
where he assumed
the rights of the first-born.

Thirty-two years on,
in the wake of an acid trip,
my thoughts mimicked
the dynamics of a game of tennis
- one where I'd only been a spectator.

Gypsies 08.17.39

My mother used to coax me
to the Westchester Avenue market,
under the el, when I was three.
Once, when I started *acting up*,
she had to drag me there,
past punnets of flowers
mocking the mean Bronx streets.

She threatened to hand me
over to the gypsies,
who were squatting in a shop
with bedspread-covered windows,
if I didn't behave.
I ignored her, so she pretended
to carry out her threat,
frog-marching me to their door
and stopping just short of opening it.
It put the fear of God into me, but
it was her way of controlling me,
and who am I to judge her?

She had been dismayed
to discover she was pregnant,
in early middle age,
later claiming to be delighted
when she first set eyes
on *the beautiful baby,* (me).
Brother Charlie told me how
he'd flipped two black
abortion pills - left to keep

cool on a window ledge -
into the yard below.
This allowed him to claim
some credit for my existence.
(An apocryphal story?)

I had stymied my mother's future,
her will to independence.
She'd already raised three kids,
but now found herself looking at
the false dawn of her liberation
through prison bars,
like *Dumbo's* mother.
While we were watching that scene
in the cinema, she told me,
rather wickedly, and to great
effect, that I would not
miss her after she died,
binding me to her with survivor's guilt.

So I was her little millstone
and she became mine.
She would put my dinner on
the table, after her day's work,
with the words, *Here's a dish*
fit for the King of Greece.
I threaded needles for her
while we listened to the radio
and talked late into the evening.

I became her confidant
and she treated me like royalty,
as Greek mothers do.

She was more than
a good enough mother,
but I will carry the unease
of the unwelcome guest
- the gypsy's stigma -
to the end of my days.

She almost won the day 09.02.39

She almost won the day,
that evening, over dinner.
She swore it was steak
but I knew better.
It was liver.
Gagging at the smell of it,
I pushed my plate away,
but she insisted and I kept
refusing
until she gave up…
for a while.

When she *did* cook steak,
it was the stringy kind
that had to be boiled,
which wasn't as bad as the
liver,
not as repulsive
though repulsive
all the same.

I told her it disgusted me,
but she kept nagging at me
to try some
after cutting it into little
pieces
and not taking no for an
answer:
until she almost had her way.
But she didn't.

Charlotte russe 02.03.40

There is a flooded cell
in my brain
that holds the
immutable
memory of
my first
Charlotte Russe.

Brother Charlie
bought it for me
in a bakery
next door to the
Star movie theatre
on Southern Boulevard,
near Hunt's Point.

The thick cream
closed my eyes
when I tongued into
a layer of
softest
sponge cake
in a paper tube.

The movies were dull,
featuring black-and-
white-hatted cowboys.
(No prize for guessing
who the good guys were.)

The serial beforehand,
typically, left
Batman trapped
in a locked cell,
and up to his chin
in rising water.

Then there was
the boring feature film,
ending in
a boring chase.

I thought,
It must get
better than this,
but I was wrong.

Singing for paperclips 02.23.40

I remember singing for paperclips
in *Hearns* department store
on Third Avenue in the Bronx.
Both of you, mother and sister,
were my mothers, each holding a hand,
as if to unravel the enigma
of the unwanted child between you.

The air was charged with oestrogen
undercut by Elizabeth Arden's *Bluegrass*.
Wilting with boredom, I waited
while you rummaged among the bargains.
Worse, those insufferable hours before,
standing on the *General Electric*
washing machine, while you, my sister,
fashioned spit curls in my hair.

The salesladies coaxed me into singing
with fistfuls of paperclips. I reprised,
You Are My Sunshine, over and over.
And every time I *did*, the ladies
added to the pile, loading
my pockets with a fool's fortune,
before we left that palace of plenty.

End of the universe 03.17.40

When it grew unbearable,
I begged her to stop,
but she wouldn't…

I, in turn, martyred the family tortoise.
I'd set it on a wringer-guard,
scavenged from the washing machine,
touch two live wires to it
and make the turtle jump
into the air with a pop.
Curiously no one stopped me.
Maybe nobody noticed.
My older brother
- sixteen at the time -
brought the turtle to school
and dissected it in biology.
It may have been sacrificed
to keep the rest of us
from killing each other.

I shared a room with another brother
when I was four, and he, fifteen.
Charlie kept marijuana and a gun
in a table between our beds.

I used to dream my body was
expanding like a balloon.
When fit to burst,
it would shrink into a pinhead,
only to expand again, and so on.

Was this a memory of enemas,
or of the beginning and end
of the universe, the *Big Bang*
and the *Big Crunch,*
or something else altogether?

Pompadour 05.12.40

The barber cut my dirty-
blonde hair short,
leaving a *Frank*
Sinatra pompadour
over the forehead,
before my father
took his turn in
the chromium chair.

We walked home
smelling of *Bay Rum*
in the *dreamtime*
East Bronx streets,
up five flights
and into the crucible
of my beginnings.

It was meant to be
an all-American
bonding experience
…except we didn't.

Anthropophobia 07.08.40

I machine-gunned my aunt
along with her teenage daughters
when I was four.
She wasn't really an aunt,
but your childhood
friend from Greece.
My toy gun not being handy,
I used my dick instead,
running past the shrinking trio
and strafing them from
beneath short trousers.
They spilled their thick
Greek coffees and glasses of water
holding spoonfuls of quince jam.
You were mortified,
but that wasn't the end of it.
I found my tin Japanese
machine-gun and returned
to massacre the lot.

Anthropophobia - a logical
mindset at the time.
I learned to hate the Japs
the Wops and the Krauts.
But I envied them, as well,
choosing to play
a Japanese soldier
in our war games,
perhaps to mimic
my ambivalence;
more likely, to conjure

a sneaky part of myself:
the despoiler I so treasured.

Every American carries a gun
in his head, as every American
has a gun to his head
- or is it a dick?
Hatred of the other might have
beat loving kindness in survival value,
out there, on the prairies,
when a yielding continent
was penetrated by hungry men.

I cared little for my “aunt” or for her
daughters, and I only wanted
to leave my mark on them,
to bind myself with my victims,
in a thrall of sex and death.

Medusa 07.11.40

I used to look down
at a brick wall
across the street,
staring at it for hours
or checking it out
from time to time
for no good reason.
I still see that wall
on Simpson Street
when I try to picture
myself as I was then.

I was the wall, the wall *me*.
Every variation of the sun,
whose death-rays
eclipsed the spirit,
hardened me into concrete
as I became the bricks
and mortar of an afternoon.

I can barely remember
the apartment, (aside from
my graffiti on the bedroom wall),
as my heart lived in the street.
At home, it felt like
a fallen tombstone
covered in undecipherable
hieroglyphics.
So I discovered my vocation
was to be like granite,

unmoved, unmoving,
born to endure the turmoil
all around me, like a rock
witnessing the spirit
of one age bleeding
into the coming of another.

In my halfway house,
the maniacs within were
informed by those without.
Blessed with my family's
peculiar love, I kept
its deadly secrets.

On my first day at school
the teacher told us to stop
whatever we were doing
when she struck
a cadence on the piano.
I went back to building my
wall of wooden bricks.
The teacher played the chords,
but I played-on,
as the other children
turned to stone.

Coda 07.12.40

I awoke from a dream of rare delight,
a forgotten mode of being.
The peace of the moment
figured in limpid tints,
the air refracting a bright
white coral turquoise clarity.
An air of infinite ease
buoying the business of being,
like dusk on the surface of a lake.
Beneath the waters
the dark-eyed wisdom of those
whose enduring love is undeniable.
It was good to remember
that madhouse childhood
was only part of the story.

After the hurricane 08.11.40

After the hurricane,
the insane Greek woman
showed us a hole the lightning
had ripped out of her ceiling.
My mother said it was God's
punishment for her evil ways.
All the same, she left me
in the woman's charge.
I gaped at the sky, glowering,
like God, into her living room.

We went into the kitchen, where
she brought a steak out of the fridge,
and started wringing it out.
The blood streamed through
her fingers into a water glass.
Then she pressed the glass
against my pursed lips,
insisting it was good for me.

Forewarned she was a witch,
I knew the crazy old woman
was another who would
not take no for an answer,
and that she wanted
to have me in her power.
I was rescued by my mother,
who walked in and broke the spell
just as I was about to drink the blood
- though I still wonder whether
I didn't swallow it, after all.

Queen of heaven 10.05.40

Tina was the daughter
of the mad woman
who lived next door.
She was thirteen
and she rarely visited.

That evening, Tina paid
me a lot of attention.
I'd never known
such intensity before
and I recognised it as
a powerful form of magic,
without anyone
having to tell me.
Then she whispered
her stupendous proposition,
like blue stars into my ear.

We slipped behind net curtains.
I just had time to notice
a majestic moon
behind veiled clouds,
casting its light down
on to that Queen of Heaven.
My mother, ever Argos-eyed,
appeared in the doorway
and spoiled the fun.
This was to be the matrix of my
every future disappointment.

Walking florence home 11.14.40

The moon was out and
she was talking about
the new confection
with great passion.
The company she
worked for hadn't yet
put it on the market,
but my brother was getting it
hot off the presses:
the chocolate pudding
was out of this world.
I tried to imagine
something
better than anything
I'd ever tasted.

Street-lamps
flickered on over
the East Bronx.
A plane floated across
an incandescent sky,
heading for LaGuardia.
Florence held forth,
with my brother dwelling
on her every word.
I was only a fly
on the wall:
there
to record the moment.

How that evening
got hard-wired into
my head is a mystery.
It has hovered
just below the horizon
of my consciousness,
over the years,
to emerge from
time to time,
inviting me to make
something of it.

At four-and-a-half,
could I have envied
the two would-be lovers?
I probably did,
craving something,
half-understood,
yet greatly desired.

Whatever it was,
insisted it be set down:
the earnest young woman
talking about chocolate,
her solicitous friend,
my brother, me,
and the indelible moment.

Singing lessons 12.14.40

Glass necks and singing lessons on Riverside Drive
where I waited for my sister,
holding Venetian glass animals to the sun,
(crushed glass and the blood of chrysanthemums);
dusty operatic Saturday afternoons.
I told Larry my sister was a diva,
and he told his sister. I got caught-out
when they met. After the war,
Larry's sister married a supermarket baron,
who didn't have a lot of time for her.
Mine married a rancher who looked
like a movie star, maybe not a star,
but a leading character actor, who talked
like Carl Rogers, rather than Roy.
I think my sister had all the luck.
The singing lessons happened when I was four.
The war came and the ladies stopped singing.

Something terrible 12.07.41

The new corner shop with the blue
stone front is never going to open.
The workmen have packed
their tools and disappeared.
Suddenly we're playing
Americans and Japs
instead of Cowboys and Indians.

Something terrible has happened.
A strange and powerful force
has stamped a purposeful
look on people's faces.
Fear and excitement is in the air.
It has dived down from heaven,
leapt up from hell, to sink
its talons into every meaning.

December darkens the pavements,
whipping the wind around
the stone-blue corner where we played,
dispersing our beginnings forever.
We stand outside the temple of our birth,
pretending nothing has happened.

Fool's gold 03.10.42

I used to ride a red
scooter to a vacant lot
around the corner,
taking along a bottle
of sugared orange juice,
not for sustenance,
but to pretend
I needed provisions
for a long perilous journey.
Typically, I went alone,
played alone, hammering
fool's gold out of the rocks.

Nowadays I drive to Hyde Park
or Hampstead Heath,
carrying a manuscript.
There, I stop to knock it
into shape over coffee.
Sometimes sparks fly.
More often, they don't,
and I am left with the dross
of so much wasted effort.
This is true alchemy.

Soula on the telephone 05.08.42

Is that you, George? your voice 6,000 miles away,
the time and space warp even greater,
as though you'd opened 20,000 doors before
making your entrance like a diva.
Wartime sister from Great Falls, Montana,
surrogate mother of the forties, only
you call me by my childhood name, now.
You come on with, *George, do you remember...?*
Suddenly I'm six to your eighteen.
The family apocrypha would have it,
we'd seen three double features in a day,
and dropped the last of your first
pay check beating it up in Schraffts.
Asked if you had any money left, you pulled out
a penny. I said, *Good, then I can weigh myself.*

Oil and sawdust 11.16.42

At 6, I learned
to impersonate a sane person.
I couldn't learn to read,
nor could I piss as high
as the Jewish boys, who had
the benefit of circumcision.

I rejected the words and letters
on the giant *Dick and Jane* book,
which the teacher jabbed at
with a torturer's pointed stick.

The oil-and-sawdust
hallways sucked the soul
right out of me, as did
my mother's American cheese
and mustard sandwiches.

Though I wanted to tear the heart
out of everyone around me,
I pretended I didn't.
After all, I was sane, like you
and me, and everybody else.

11.28.07

Under the stairs 02.14.43

Kisses under the stairs.
She wanted Dominic's,
not mine,
so I had to bribe her
with sweets to get one.
I shook off the rejection,
thinking it better
to buy a kiss
than to have none at all.
Precocious, *n'est-ce-pas?*
My mother had lied.
I would never be the envy
of them all, *not* the best.
That Dominic was,
was hard to take,
but Janet forced home this
truth with her refusal.

She moved away soon afterwards,
and we met by chance,
twelve years later,
in a Catskills hotel
where I was working
as a holiday photographer
during the summer break.
She'd become a sumptuous,
blue-eyed, blonde of eighteen
- an American Monica Vitti -
and her skin had acquired
a remarkable glow.

We met under my photos
of people eating chicken.
She smiled fetchingly
and gazed at me with
those tender eyes.
Janet said she would have
gone out with me,
but she was engaged
to a promising medical student.
It was serious.
I was not the best.

The fridge 04.23.44

I fell for it - locking
myself in the fridge
to see if the light went
out when the door closed.
I emptied it before I
got in, overlooking
a small plate of *bacalao,*
salted cod, whose pungency
has followed me around
the world ever since.
The light went out, all right,
and I was trapped like so
many before and after.
It wouldn't open from
the inside, like today's fridges
with their magnetic catches.

Tabloid headlines of my death
flashed through my head.
I tried shouting for help,
knowing my father,
who worked at night,
asleep three rooms away,
would never hear me.
In a desperate bid to survive,
I broke the plate, using
a shard to hack away at the
rubber seal around the door
and pressed my nose
against the crack for air.

Hearing me shout on
his way to the bathroom,
my father opened the door.
He just stood there
in his boxer shorts,
in open-mouthed amazement.
He didn't seem particularly
pleased to have rescued me.

Then again, his own father
had thrown him down a well
when he was fourteen.
So he ran away
and spent ten years criss-
crossing the world in
the belly of freighters.
There is a photograph of him
and three other sailors,
dressed as devils, holding
pitchforks, taken the first
time he crossed the equator.

We used to bailout the
submarine, our rowboat,
which we found submerged
every Sunday morning.
We would row from City
Island to Orchard Beach,
in felicitous silence,
under a mother-of-pearl sky,
enclosing us, as within an oyster,
like the inside of that fridge.

Duende 06.06.44

We were visiting a friend
of my mother's, in a house
still mapped somewhere
on the left side of my brain.
I had a tapeworm, and
I'd been given a purgative
to flush the thing out,
and I rushed to the bathroom
the minute we got there.
I was aghast when I felt
the tapeworm emerging.
My mother grabbed-hold of it,
yanked it free and flushed it
down the toilet, spitting
in its wake as it disappeared.

The tapeworm was Satan.
She'd seen him before and
knew how to deal with him.
Some lives later,
I became that tapeworm,
languishing in my own
bowels, in a dream
- a defensive strategy
whose cons eventually
outweighed the pros...

Though I no longer labour
under this phantasy,
I sometimes try

to become Satan again
- just for a night -
and I make it, now and then

Jewish holidays 10.26.44

On Jewish holidays my school
took on a desultory abandoned air,
with the odd Irish or Italian kid
sulking in a desert of chairs.
The lessons were non-existent,
so, half-a-century later,
I ask why I bothered to go to
school at all on those days.
To feel deprived for not being Jewish?
To waste my time, completely
- a lesson learned and assiduously
applied, as when I avoided the draft?
To grasp the true meaning of the term,
chosen people: they, whose children
feast on apples and nuts at the Seder,
and on crackly unleavened bread
on yet another holiday in the spring?

I envied those anointed children
- with their long summer camp vacations -
almost to the point of resentment.
They wore more fashionable clothes,
their fathers had newer bigger cars,
(in our case, any car at all).
They moved out of the old
neighbourhood into suburban homes,
as soon as they could, after the war,
(the Jewish emigration, which started
earlier than that of Southern Europe,
having put them one step ahead of us).

Languishing in a near-empty classroom
had a familiar feel for me,
revisited in a dream, where I
was sitting in an empty caravan,
off the coast of Brittany.
There, I considered my hate/love
of the infernal/delightful French
- not to mention, people in general.
A sense of being unconnected.
Part of no community.
Denying the reality of the other.
A situation I still deal with.
Luxuriating in the anonymity
of a callous city, I call *home*.
Most of all, no connection.

Pigeon’s milk 11.27.44

When I was eight I had
a Saturday job helping-out
on a subway station flower stall.
The boss seemed O.K.
until he sent me out to buy
a quart of pigeon's milk.
It was my third week.
(Now everybody knows
pigeons don't give milk,
but this did not occur
to me at the time.)
The boss split his sides
when I came back
empty-handed from the dairy.
I didn't want to be the butt
of any more so called *pranks*,
so I flew the coop.
                                        Instead,
I had a go at shining shoes.
I hardly needed the money;
I only wanted to partake of
the alchemy of turning
nothing into dollars.
I made a shoeshine box
and touted for business under
the same elevated subway station.
But I was soon fed-up with
holding a begging bowl.

One afternoon I saw my father
lurching out of that station.
He was home late from work,
and royally drunk, staggering
down Kingsbridge Road,
barely able to keep from falling.
I felt ashamed of him
and of myself, because I couldn't
cross that road to help him...

Pigeon's milk, shoe polish,
and a helpless father.
Rancid memories they may be,
but they are mine.

Opting out 12.13.44

Faking a stomach-ache
to get off school
- mother, bless her,
needed no convincing -
I took to my bed
with cups of Lipton's tea
thin cut marmalade
soda crackers and a radio.
Then I killed the morning
listening to anything
while I waited for
The Green Hornet
Boston Blackie
and *The Shadow*.

My father slept until
four in the afternoon,
when the old sailor
rose to a glass
of lemon juice and water.
After a slow shave,
he rode the subway
all the way to Jersey City,
sweating-out the night
beside a baker's oven.

Delight came at five
with the children's serials,
the detective and
the comedy shows

that peopled my solitude:
The Lone Ranger
Gangbusters
The Whistler and
The Thin Man.

Do you remember
what happened every time
Molly opened
Fibber McGee's
closet?
You probably don't.

Porcupines 02.16.45

It began when my sister
sent me out for a box of *Modess*.
On the way, I met a kid
I hardly knew, who asked
if I wanted to run away
from home with him.
Without hesitating, I said *yes*.
(I still don't know why.
Was I more embarrassed
about my errand than I
realised at the time?
Did I jump at the chance
to act-out my alienation?)
I met the kid on the corner
after delivering the sanitary towels
and with nothing more than
the change from the drugstore
in my pocket, we ran away.

We took the IRT from
Kingsbridge Road to Woodlawn
and Van Courtland Park
- the last stop, though only
three stations down the line.
Feeling hungry when we got off,
I pushed my last pennies
into a peanut machine
on the platform.
The park held memories
of picnics where Greek families

roasted lamb over charcoal
to the sound of a clarinet
weaving into the warp
of a Sunday afternoon.
It looked different now,
as we walked into the darkness.
We began to feel uneasy
- my friend even more than I.

He started to panic when we
tried to settle down for the night
in a hollow in the middle of a field.
He asked me if porcupines
really shot their quills.
I said they didn't, (hopefully).
The prospect of being attacked
by animals with glowing eyes
took a grip on my mind.
We tried to get to sleep in the
dew-drenched grass, but as we
were cold scared and hungry,
we gave up almost right away.
The glamour of running away
had palled for the both of us.
I didn't argue when my friend
said he wanted to go home.

We made our way out of the park,
alert to the threat of porcupines
and walked home, through streets
more perilous than the park itself.

As we neared the neighbourhood,
I could hear my mother calling my name.
She'd been looking for me for hours.
Luckily, relief at finding me
had cancelled-out her anger...
The porcupine became a totem of
defensive fury mixed with fear,
which I embodied from that night on,
when the occasion called for it,
though I eventually learned
to live without it.

Joe dimaggio died today 08.07.45

Joe DiMaggio died today.
This took me back
to the morning after Hiroshima.
Johnny and I were drunk with
the bomb to end all bombs
that filled the newspapers
and energised the airways.
It was the most exciting thing
that had happened in our
nine years on the planet,
ending the war and heralding
the end of childhood lived
in war's triumphant shadow.
So many killed with such science
and for a just cause, we were told.

That day we learned
of a tiny entity
which could be split to produce
an unimaginable explosion.
Johnny and I threw nickels
against the sidewalk
all morning, as hard
as we could, hoping
to repeat the experiment...

Five, the American number,
my lucky number
as on a nickel
as on DiMaggio's shirt

as in Paul Duluth's painting, No.5
as in Nineteen Forty-Five.

The bomb was all everyone
talked about that August.
I was the first kid on the block
to send away for an atom bomb
ring from a *Cheerios* packet.
It was a small aluminium
cylinder with black plastic fins
fixed onto an adjustable ring.
I stood in a darkened closet,
popped the tail fins off
and peered through the lens,
to see the random firing
of radium particles within.

It was a rare spectacle,
rarer than the radium itself,
like the miracle of the United States
and that of the New York Yankees
and of the power for which they stand.
I was witnessing the end of time
and sharing a prescient guilt
with my predator country:
DiMaggio demolishing the Tigers
in the bottom of the ninth
in a segue of annihilation,
not unlike the Dervish atoms' dance.

03.08.99

Harvey's mother 04.19.46

Every afternoon Harvey's mother
called time on our street games
to give Harvey a banana.
Harvey didn't like bananas
and he often threw-up in protest.
On the street he was a near-
invincible artful dodger and
sleight-of-hand artist. No one
could pin him down in any game.

One day I passed on the
misinformation, hot off
the presses, that babies were
made with the aid of scumbags,
rather than the contrary.
The following afternoon
while he was at Schule,
where Jewish kids went
to learn Hebrew after school,
his mother called me from
their first-floor window.
I went into their apartment
for the first time.

She brought me to the bathroom,
where she was bathing Harvey's
little brother and confronted me:
Harvey said you told him
something dirty, yesterday, she began,
her voice becoming impossibly shrill.

Is this child dirty? Is he?

I was thrown by the shock
and the shame of it.
She screamed again, *Is he dirty? Is he?*
I guess she had a lot to scream about.

The lady or the tiger 05.20.46

I was in Mrs Hector's class for years.
Fearsome unsmiling and somewhat desiccated,
she was in her fifties and worthy of her name.
I was an indifferent student; I didn't fit in
with the purposeful ethos of that school,
(or of *any* school, for that matter).
Mrs Hector warmed to me when I showed
signs of talent in the writing department.
My first poem, at ten, began with the
sound of horses' hooves on cobblestones
and it ended with an image of the
moon glinting on frozen tiled roofs.
That's all I can remember, except for
the sheer excitement of writing it.
It had the authenticity of a persistent
memory left over from a previous life.

I became her reluctant protégé,
miraculously winning her approval,
while enjoying myself at the same time.
Mrs Hector got us to invent endings
for stories that had ambiguous conclusions,
such as *The Legend of Sleepy Hollow*.
One day she asked us to finish
a story called *The Lady or the Tiger*.
It was a tale of gladiatorial combat
in the presence of a king,
who would reward the winner with
the hand of his daughter or the jaws of a tiger.
The original left the reader in the dark
about which the king would choose.

Although my version hinted
that the gladiator would get the lady,
I had the king give him the thumbs-down
- and the tiger - in the end.
Mrs Hector was so outraged by the
sheer perversity of my conclusion,
that she threw my story back at me.
I discovered that ambivalence upsets people
like practically nothing else - especially, teachers.

I scream 07.12.46

I spent two weeks with
a paranoid old lady
and her paranoid
middle-aged son.
They lived in a house
in the country
in Lake Carmel, N.Y.
The old lady, who had
invited me to stay with them,
worked alongside my mother
stuffing toys in a sweatshop
in midtown Manhattan.

Lake Carmel was practically
at the end of the garden.
The son kept a large
metal rowboat there.
He would take me out
on the lake and tell me
how much he hated commies.

They had two nieces, twins,
slightly younger than myself,
also staying with them.
The smell of piss predominated
in that house as the nieces
wet their beds every night.
The girls didn't seem able
to express themselves otherwise:
at least, we never spoke
to one-another.

Dysfunction was everywhere.
When I left my clothes behind
in the bathroom after a shower,
I heard the son shout to his mother,
in the next room, for me to hear,
Did you see how Georgie left his
underwear lying around?
I was mortified, and had I stayed
with them for the whole summer,
I would have ended up seriously damaged.

Otherwise they would be chillingly
cheerful: when the ice cream
van pulled up, they would chant,
I scream,
you scream,
we all scream
for ice cream.
Another treat was potato bread,
made of wheat and potato flour.
Unheard-of in the city,
it seemed exotic to me.

I played with a girl my age,
called Violet. My brother,
who came up for the day,
called her *Violent*
- but she wasn't really.
She became the object
of my 12-year-old phantasies,
(though she was a tomboy,
and we kept each other

at a schoolyard distance).
Too bad.

I came to visit for the day,
a few years later,
with my friend, Stevie,
(whose father really
was a Communist).
The middle-aged son
took us out on the lake
in his metal boat,
and let loose an hour-long
anti-Communist tirade.

Stevie and I and this hateful
redneck in the same boat.
I felt embarrassed that Stevie
might think I had such a person
for a friend - it was almost
as bad as leaving behind
my underwear in the bathroom.
(As I said, this man and his
mother were a dysfunctional lot.)

Sweating quarters 10.25.46

Selling tickets for the American Nautical
Cadets' raffle to earn a decommissioned rifle,
I hit on the idea of pitching to a captive
audience on subways cars, between stations.
Ten-years-old, and kitted-out for the role
in sailor's suit and white spats,
(which I scrubbed at the last minute
every Friday night, wearing them
to the meetings, dripping wet),
I charmed quarter after quarter from the crowd.

What was this magic all about?
Unable to be myself, I discovered
my metier was to be a salesman.
I began to walk around with false
good posture that hid my thoughts
but was approved of by teachers.
The Commander was fond of punishing
his young recruits on general principle.
He would make them hold out a rifle,
at arms length, for agonizing minutes.
I only had to do this once
but I won't forget how my arms ached,
the newly washed spats sticking,
clammily, on to constricted ankles.

We never got near a ship.
Instead, we played war
games in Van Courtland Park.
I became skilful at evading capture,

sometimes falling asleep behind a bush,
waiting for someone to surrender to.
I grew to hate the cadets
with their authoritarian ethos
which appealed to those
who longed for discipline
and I was relieved when I quit,
my only happy memory being that of
sweating quarters from the crowd.

Snow 12.05.46

I'd borrow the super's snow shovel
and tout my services to shopkeepers,
clearing snow from pavements
all along Kingsbridge Road.
I charged twenty-five cents,
the price of a kitten from a pet shop.
I didn't need the money,
just the cover of an entrepreneurial
role to hide behind, already, at ten.
The work was hard when the snow
was impacted, had thawed, was trod
upon by multitudes, froze again.
I'd warm-up with a hot chocolate,
wring-out my socks and go back out.
In near-blizzards I could lose myself
in the interstices of an alternative
white universe, blown away with the
snow streaming across city intersections.

One Saturday, I worked my way
down from Kingsbridge Road to
Third Avenue and Fordham.
I bought a small kitten from a pet shop,
though I knew my mother
would refuse it houseroom.
She was superstitious about black cats.
I pleaded my case, pointing out a miniscule
tuft of white fur just under its chin
and was surprised when she let me keep it,
(which was the kitten's bad luck).

I clipped its whiskers to find out if cats
really needed them to locate nearby objects.
Then followed a sadistic *experiment*
to see whether the kitten would
land on its feet when bundled
in a bag and pushed off a table.
(I know children sometimes
do this sort of thing, but I still
wince at the memory.)
When I consider my daughter, surrounded
by totems of her own goodness, by way
of soft toy animals and living pets,
I mourn that ten-year-old boy
and seek his absolution.
My evil
conversion into victim is another story.
I became this victim to be
distanced from the torturer.
But I was both. When I hid behind
the victim, I denied my life's blood.
I looked for some way out of
this scenario of neglect and indifference,
some kind of whiteout ending.
I wanted to love enough
those I had taken into my life
and who had invited me into theirs'.

My mother gave away the kitten,
which was its first stroke of luck.
At least I hope it was, this kitten
with a white tuft, banked,
like snow, beneath its chin.

Mock execution 12.10.46

Flanagan, the janitor's son,
lured me into a disused shop,
along with his accomplice,
a younger kid who lived next
door to him in the basement.
I still can't see how I
fell for it, even at ten.
We scrambled through a hole
in the roof onto a scene
covered in the dust of ages,
untouched since before the war
- a set out of Cocteau's *Orphée.*
*An el*ectric chair stood
in the middle of the room.
Made of four-by-fours and
leather straps, with wire coiling-off,
it looked authentic enough.
After we dropped through,
they grabbed me and firmly
strapped me into the chair.

Flanagan told me I was
about to be electrocuted.
Then they began to toy with me.
Flanagan gave me the chance
to speak my last words,
if I could think of any.
I could see it was my despair
that made his eyes light up

with the joy of the hangman.
We'd seen it all before
in the movies, and everyone
played his role, condemned,
executioner and lackey.

Flanagan went to hit the switch,
then hesitated, before they both
broke into spiteful laughter.
Then they loosened the straps
and let me go.
Flanagan was sixteen,
headed for a jailbird's life, perhaps,
and I for better things, (I hoped),
the lucky son of a baker,
who lived on the fifth floor.

Butter 12.16.46

The argument was over whether *Sutters*
used butter in their baking,
as they claimed, rather than shortening.
(*Sutters* was a fancy local bakery.)
In those days we all believed
lots of butter was good for you.
It was hard to come by
during the war, but my father
always managed to find a pound
or two on the black-market.

Our geography teacher
was convinced they didn't.
Her name was Ann,
though we never called her that.
She was Catholic-Irish
and grossly overweight.
I christened her *Paint-Bucket Annie*,
imagining her periods to be so
copious, she would need a paint-
bucket to contain them.
We'd only recently found
out about menstruation.

I set her straight over the butter.
My father, who was a baker, judged
that *Sutters'* cake was made with it.
My contradicting her enraged the teacher.
Her eyes narrowed when she said,
Just because your father owns some

two-bit bakery doesn't mean he's right!
I was at a loss, a ready subject
for an easy put-down.

Swept away by the winds of emotion,
I half-believed what she was saying.
Half of me wanted to disappear,
like Kipling's tiger turning into butter,
into the red earth of India
on the map beside the blackboard.
The other half wanted to get over it,
and I *did*...somewhat...eventually.

The minotaur 06.18.47

Cab Calloway singing
It Ain't Necessarily So
on the phonograph.
The Empire State Building
glinting in the distance
through my fifth-floor
bedroom window.
I am fashioning a knobbly-
kneed statuette of
Don Quixote out of solder.
Not bad, I think,
for a first effort.
What does Cab
mean when he sings,
old Pharaoh's daughter
fished Moses, she SAYS,
from that stream?
My room is heavy
with solder-flux, and the
kitchen with strawberries.
Nick puts *La Boheme*
on the phonograph.

The sun, setting over
New Jersey, slants into
the apartment through
south-facing windows.
The light of Genoa gives
over to the light of Bilbao
in the evening breeze.
I hold a baseball glove

to my face and take-in
a lungful of oiled leather.
I can hear my mother
frying lamb chops
before the odour drifts
in from the kitchen.

My brother, Nick,
is suddenly furious with me
over some small misdemeanour.
His anger stumps me
because I want to be
close to him, which
is proving impossible.
Mimi is dying again.
I feel rubbished by
my savage super-ego
(that is, my brother).
Embracing the bullying,
I promise not to do again
whatever it was I had done
to anger him.

The record player
clatters to a stall.
We sit down to supper
in the thick atmosphere
of a fry-up.
I crucify my brother
in my mind,
grunting through his food
from across the table,
in the centre of the Labyrinth.

Montana 07.22.47

I walked in my sleep
on the first night in Montana,
waking to find myself
on the cold metal seat of a
John Deere tractor
in my underwear
in the middle of the night
in the middle of a field
on the prairies.
I was just eleven.
My sister's house was
bathed in moonlight,
a quarter-of-a-mile away.
I fought my fear enough
to make it back to the house.
Almost my first night away
from New York City.
After I got over the emptiness,
the endless space, kerosene lamps,
(even the washing machine ran on gasoline),
a towering boredom closed-in
from all directions, like a land-borne
tsunami which threatened the void.
But I was used to being on my own.

The nearest house was miles away.
It belonged to two old-
timers, Jack and Timothy.
They were life-long bachelors
who hadn't changed their ways
since homesteading times,

except for their radio, which was
hooked-up to an old car battery.
One of them seemed bitter,
the other predominantly sad.
Dry land farming is a hard life…
They told apocryphal stories about
Montana during the depression,
such as the night they were caught short
in Great Falls, fifty miles away.
They risked their last
silver dollar in a poker game,
willing it to win them the price
of a hotel room - which it did…

One afternoon, addled with boredom,
I climbed on Jack's white horse,
rode him bareback out of the corral
and on to the open fields.
The horse had a habit of biting Jack
on the shoulder, given the chance,
for which reason Jack hated him.
I'd never ridden a horse before, but
I'd often seen it done in the movies.
The animal trundled along peacefully
for about ten minutes, until the son-
of-a-bitch decided to head for home.
He turned around and made for the stables
at full gallop, jumping fences along the way.
Lacking a saddle, stirrups or bridle,
I hung on to the horse's mane for dear life
in the middle of a field,
in the middle of the afternoon,
on the prairie, in Montana.

Lavina 07.29.47

July, Nineteen-Forty-Seven.
I was eleven and Lavina was in her twenties.
My sister and her husband
had gone to Great Falls for the day,
driving fifty miles over dirt roads.
Lavina and I were thrown together,
so we spent the afternoon smoking
and drinking Miller High Life.
We found excitement in each other's company,
while her husband Leonard was one-waying the fields.
There wasn't another house for miles and Brady,
the closest town, was twenty-five miles away.

We both needed company. It was practically my
first time outside of New York City.
She was so different from anyone I'd ever met.
She also seemed out of place,
with her beginnings in the Deep South.
She was married to an older man
who didn't pay her much attention.
Leonard's life had almost certainly been hard.
He was a practical man in his forties.
I was shocked when I saw him sprinkle their mattress
with DDT the day they arrived, though this
must have been the custom among migrant farmhands.

Lavina was a good storyteller, but
she seemed starved of an audience.
I guessed she was bored with Leonard, she acted
so pent-up and in need of self-expression.

On the other hand, she just liked talking,
after spending endless days waiting
in a stranger's house for her husband
to come in for lunch, for dinner.
She told tales of wild goings-on in southern
country graveyards, peopled with her many
brothers, punctuated with smoke and drink.
Lavina spoke with a disarming bluntness.
She spoke with real immediacy, unlike me.
I hid behind alienated posturings.
Her eyes and her body danced to story
upon story, pure energy high-jacking her will.
Lavina and the words she spoke were one.

She seemed ready for anything.
The forbidden beer and cigarettes,
and the fact she was a grown woman,
flirting with me, tempted me
to think of planting a kiss on her lips.
She might have let me if I'd tried.
She talked on while Leonard ploughed through
the long dazzling Montana afternoon.
I liked listening to women.
I'd heard the minutiae of my mother's
and my sister's lives from my earliest beginnings.
What women claim they like best about me
is that I listen to what they have to say.

I wanted that afternoon to last,
for Leonard to keep on ploughing,
for my sister to stay in Great Falls,
and for Lavina and I to go on talking
in that beery smoky kitchen.

But the afternoon ended and we
never repeated the experience.
Afterwards, I turned her into an object of fun,
calling her *Latrina*, (not to her face),
and mocking her southern ways,
because she'd charmed me,
and I had no way of dealing with it.

Bully 03.28.48

I thought of him today at 3 in the afternoon.
That's when he would lie in wait for me,
on my way home from P.S. 86. The bully.
A gangling boy of thirteen, the son of an
Irish-Catholic janitor on my street,
University Avenue in the Bronx.
He'd stretch-out a long freckled arm
to bar my way and push me down
on to the pavement by his tenement wall.

He never said what he was after.
I guess he just wanted
to force his will on any*one*
and any*thing* - *especially me* -
to make me squirm, (which I
always did, afraid of what
might follow if I resisted).
Deprived of my will, I felt
a powerful sense of despair.
In an instant, I'd become
his plaything inside the gates of Hell.
He'd let me go after 10 or 15 minutes,
when he was either gratified or bored.

This went on for months.
Perhaps he lost interest, or maybe
I found another route home.
I can't remember which.
I like to think I confronted him,
but I probably didn't.

The poor kids in our neighbourhood
had a ferocious need to dominate.
Curiously, when I try to picture his
long-jawed angular freckled face, now,
I see the face of Charles Bukowsky.

Comics 05.12.48

I invited her up to my room
to trade comic books.
And she accepted. I asked her
not to tell her mother,
and she agreed. In my mind
it was an assignation.

She was Irish and brash.
I can see her freckled face,
and her pigtails
falling on either shoulder.
If I'm not mistaken,
her name was Patricia.
Of course I'm not mistaken,
only embarrassed I can
still remember it.

In the intervening days
I was lost in phantasy,
struggling to imagine
what it might be like
to explore a female body.

I hid my favourite Captain Marvels,
all the same, in case she might
covet them and turn them
into the currency of a kiss.

On the chosen afternoon, I ran
into her mother on the street.

Her face said it all.
It was no longer kindly, no longer
pleased to see the *nice* kid
she'd stopped to share a moment with.
I'd become a shifty, calculating,
tween, up to no good, (though
that word hadn't yet been coined).

Her mother knew about our plan.
She'd once told her daughter
that if anyone said not to
tell her mother something,
she should do so immediately.
So she did. It seems reasonable
advice now, but it didn't then

BLT down 06.06.48

I would order a BLT down
and a brown cow, signifying
a bacon-lettuce-and-tomato
sandwich on toast with a
glass of chocolate milk.
More often it was salmon salad,
canned salmon mixed with
chopped celery and mayonnaise.
Sandwiches at the soda-fountain
luncheonette, where I went every
day when I was about twelve,
beat school meals and the brown-
bagged variety from home.
The owner let us read comics
over a sandwich, which was heaven
and eating there got me out of school.

I also escaped on Wednesday afternoons
to prepare for communion
in the Dutch Reformed Church
just around the corner.
I came away with a sense of the
power of the church, rather than
with any notion of spirituality.
The pastor was friendly, though,
and he engaged me in long
rambling conversations - unlike my
teachers, who kept themselves
at an authoritarian distance.

I went to a woodwork class there
one evening a week, taught by
a sado-erotic ex-marine
who used the setting
as an excuse to hit the boys.
He posed this problem to us:
if you were stranded on a desert
island and could have only
one tool at your disposal,
which would you choose?
After listening to us run through
a catalogue of everything you could
find in a toolbox, he eventually
told us that the answer was, *a knife.*
You could improvise a shelter
with one, hunt with it and so on.
Sometimes he'd organise a game of
Ringalevio, which allowed him
to take off his belt and whack
any hapless boy he caught.
It felt sexual then and it still does.
The severe Protestantism of that church
provided a perfect setting for this
repressed kinky sexuality.

At a Halloween party in the church
basement, I spent the evening
trying to guess whether a
fourteen-year-old in a woman's
bathing suit was male or female.
He/she refused to speak.

While we bobbed for apples
and played spooky games
but mainly sat around awkwardly,
none of us could take our eyes
off of this winsome character
posing as a beauty queen.
We never *did* find out.
Looking back, I think
it *was* a boy, whose trans-
sexual desires must have
drawn him to that schizoid milieu.

When I was older, I asked the owner
of the luncheonette for a Saturday
job as a soda jerk. He hired me,
but on my first morning he made
me get on my knees and scrub the
black marks made by rubber heels
from around the counter-stools.
I had to use steel wool and the
work was filthy - not at all what
I'd expected, which was to make
sundaes and ice-cream sodas.
Feeling exploited and betrayed,
I handed-in my apron in disgust.

A few weeks later,
his wife ran off with a salesman,
who use to call-in regularly,
which didn't surprise me.
I figured the bastard
got what he deserved.

I received communion,
which filled a vague
pre-adolescent spiritual need
stimulated by a secular childhood.
After the pastor moved to New Jersey,
I stayed away from the church
and the luncheonette, as well,
so avoiding the permanently stunned
look on the owner's face.

Baseball 06.19.48

The excitement was tangible.
I woke up at six
on the morning
of our new team's first game.
After checking out the weather,
(sunny and warm), I spent
the rest of the morning
riding the riotous energy
rising like sap within me.

We called ourselves the *Eagles*,
after an East Bronx sweatshop,
which had offered us a discount
on our uniforms,
emblazoning its name
across our chests, in return.

I'd arranged a game
with a team of
younger poorer boys,
who lived in the hinterlands
beyond the Jerome Avenue El.
I made myself manager
and played center field,
of course, like Joe DiMaggio,
leaving Harvey to do the pitching,
conceding he was better at it than I.
Once the game began,
I kept running up
to the diamond, between batters,
to coach the infielders.

My guidance was hardly needed,
as our poor deprived opponents,
(without a uniform among them,
and with pitifully little equipment),
could not play baseball.
They were worse than bad.
None of them could hit,
and their fielding was no better.

Their pathetic cheating shocked us,
when, for example, a boy
kept on running down the baseline,
between third and home,
pretending he had been at bat,
hoping to confuse us.
Beating them brought little joy.
We were the well-fed
middle class defeating
an undernourished underclass.
Their mindset was of those
who believe themselves born losers.

After the game, they tried,
half-heartedly,
to steal our bats and gloves.
(Though smaller than we,
they were meaner,
and would have beaten us
in a fight, if one had broken out.)
I went home as dejected
as I had been excited that same morning.
So ended the *Eagles'*
first and only game.

Waiting for the barbarians 06.21.48

Mrs Hector, my aptly named
primary school teacher,
would call me *impertinent*
when I disagreed with her.
Naturally, I took this word
to be synonymous with *cheeky*.

In fact, what she meant was,
You are not thinking
what I am thinking,
or, *You are not thinking*
what I want you to think.

Was she anticipating
the 21st century?
Was she anticipating
the advent of the barbarians,
the ones with the supercomputers?

She may have busted
many a young man's balls,
but she wasn't a bad sort.
What's more, her love
of literature was obvious.

So, in a way, I'm glad
to have had the thoughts
she wanted me to have
- for a while, at least -
if only to prepare me
for the present. 06.18.07

Red river valley 07.05.48

At twelve, I sold my tropical
fish and bought a record player
with Schumann's First
Symphony on six-78 records.
I also bought a big *Harmony* guitar
which I played for a couple
of years until I replaced it
with a 0018 *Martin.*
I shot an arrow through the sound-
hole of the *Harmony* the day
I brought the *Martin* home.

I took lessons from a
middle-aged Italian
who lived next to Poe's Cottage
on the Grand Concourse,
(the Bronx's Champs-Elysées).
He presumed to teach you
any instrument, whether or not
he could play it himself.
He taught me the six chords
he knew on the guitar.
I think he really played accordion.

After cutting my teeth on
Black Is The Colour, I picked up
Red River Valley from a record
by Les Paul and Mary Ford.
This melancholy number
matched my mood precisely.

I learned a lot of songs
after that, even German lieder
and Italian art songs,
accompanied by Mrs Dolgow
on a grand piano in the
tower of Seven Arts High.
overlooking Harlem.

The *Martin* served me well
through college, where
it sometimes turned into
a weapon of seduction.
At 21, I sold that guitar,
(which I later regretted),
to buy a ticket to Europe.
That *Martin* was the
truest of companions.
It tapped into my soul, so,
naturally, it had to go.

Medusa revisited 07.10.48

Daniel looked like a
twelve-year-old *Glenn Ford,*
the sculpted jaws
the handsome healthy aura and
especially the trustworthy eyes,
but his character was the
exact opposite of his looks.
To say he was hateful
would not be unfair,
only accurate.
He seethed revenge for wrongs
I could only guess at.
Later in life he told me
his ambition was to become
an exterminator, ostensibly
an exterminator of insects, but
we both understood his meaning.

His mother seemed uncertain
and nervous about child rearing.
Once, when I invited him
for supper, my mother cooked us
steak and fried potatoes.
Afterwards, when his mother
discovered he'd eaten no
green vegetables, she set
a bowl of boiled French beans
in front of him and made him
finish it, to my mortification,
(as this made me feel

my family was badly
lacking in nutritional savvy).

Daniel's twin sister Miriam soaked-up
all of his parents' affection.
She embodied their ambitions for the future.
Daniel used to pretend to tickle
her because this gave him the
opportunity to feel-her-up.
I joined-in the tickling game
one evening, when his parents
had gone off to the movies,
leaving Miriam and Daniel home.
After a while, he left us together
while he went to watch their
prototype TV, which had a thick
magnifying lens over the screen.

I was twelve and at the threshold
of my first sexual adventure,
bewildered by the vagaries of it all.
Miriam seemed to welcome my attentions,
so I initiated a game of I'll show
you mine, if you show me yours
- a game interrupted seven years
before, when my mother walked into
a room where I was almost at dalliance
with a fourteen-year-old seductress.
Miriam went along with me,
and when I showed her mine,
her eyes widened, signalling she'd
never before seen a penis in anger.

I saw Daniel peeping at us through
the crack of the slightly opened door.
He disappeared the moment our eyes met.
When it was her turn to show me hers,
she lifted her nightie and lay back
to display her sex in its entirety.
Now, I'd never seen one before and
I wasn't even sure whether the fault-
line ran vertically or horizontally,
I was so unprepared for this horrible
unnecessarily complicated spectacle.

I was transfixed by the sight of the
Medusa, a sight so repulsive,
its imagined appeal evaporated.
Hardly able to believe that such
a pretty creature as Miriam could
possess such a hideous part,
I left her to join Daniel who was
pretending to be engrossed in TV.
We sat in silence in the flickering
blue light, both of us acting
as though nothing had happened.

The green bike 07.14.48

When I was twelve,
I spray-painted
an old bike green,
in the cellar
of my father's bakery.
(It was actually
dark viridian.)

A man posing as
a delivery boy
had swindled me
out of my brand-new
shiny red *Schwinn,*
a month before.
I think I chose
its complimentary colour
to neutralize my loss,
(as well as my subsequent
envy of the thief).

The dark cellar was coated
in greasy black dust:
(not ideal conditions
for spray painting,
according to the
instructions on the can).

The result was patchy,
as you would expect,
leaving me with a furry

green bike, instead
of the shiny one
I was aiming for.

I didn't want to bring
my ridiculous bike
out of the cellar and
into the light of day,
and tried to forget it.

I set up an ice cream stand,
outside my father's bakery,
(my enterprise, entirely),
and bought stock from
a local wholesaler,
who also supplied dry ice.

But, there were pitifully
few customers,
(possibly because
my stall looked dodgy).
After a few bleak
July afternoons,
I shifted the stock
to my father's freezer,
and kissed the ice cream
business goodbye.

To boost my morale,
I treated myself to
my first homemade
flan, (crème caramel),

in the Puerto Rican diner
across the road.

It tasted good to me;
better than my ice cream.
I licked my lips
when I finished.

Then I remembered the bike.

A puritanical act 01.13.49

I can think of dozens
of times I fell foul
of my brother Nick,
but this must top the bill.

When I was 13,
I walked into my bedroom
to find my entire *Wank Bank*
spread across the bed:
the cartoon drawings
of female action heroines
in provocative poses,
ample breasts
straining leotards
- even an actual photograph
of a beckoning blonde
stretching in skin-tight cat suit.

It had been bad enough
when my mother walked in
on me while I was *at it*,
and to hear her say:
Georgie, already?
(I threw her out.)

But Nick's exposing
my secret cache
of childish erotica
was downright sinister.

His laying it all out
on my bed was
an act of Puritanism,
in every schizoid particular.
He was out to exercise power
- throw his weight around,
in any way he could.
(The guy was 26-years old!)

I got rid of my collection,
and turned instead to images
of girdle ads from the pages
of the New York Times.
I used to imagine one
or two girls from high school
wearing these risqué undergarments,
and allowing me to slip
my hand under their petticoats.

Now, Ronnie Laing once observed
that in order to masturbate
you had to be able to hold on
to an image in your mind.
He told me he had never done it,
as an adolescent,
but I hoped this wasn't true.

Ronnie's refusal to indulge himself
might go a long way towards explaining
his need to get seriously pissed
before he could walk off
with one of the groupies who stalked
him in his middle years.

When brother Charlie told me
Nick went at it like a jackhammer,
according to a woman
Charlie had fixed him up with,
I imagined Nick doing it like
an infant attacking the breast…

Meanwhile, *Wonder Woman*
and sensuous Cat Suit Woman
remain erotic presences
in my mental archaeology,
standing-in for the moment
I became transfixed by
that impossible concept,
that concept being: *SHE*.

Stevie 02.12.49

My mother called him
to kakarotsi - both him and his
Miniature Doberman pinscher.
The dog's name was *Crafty*
and it did indeed resemble
a cockroach, in a way.
That she used the same
sobriquet for Stevie was less
than charitable, but it fit.
He had one of those faces
you could only see in profile.
Looking at him head-on
made you long to widen it,
so that the features made sense.
You only had to look at his
little brother to see the handsome
face fate had robbed him of.
He also had a nervous tic
that jolted his head sideways
and sent his eyes skywards
every couple of minutes.

Stevie and I were outcasts,
relieved to have found one-another,
though he went to Horace Mann,
and I, to Seven Arts High School.
I lived in a sixth-floor apartment
on Kingsbridge Road, with a clear
view of the Empire State building,
and he in one of the few detached houses
with a garden in our neighbourhood.

On rites of passage Saturday nights
we played poker and drank
Miller High Life, getting drunk
on the first or second can.
We were also preoccupied
with keeping tropical fish - even
attending ichthyology lectures
at the *Museum on Natural History.*
It became an obsession for us both,
until I swapped my 28 fish-tanks
for a record player and *Schumann's*
First, on five twelve-inch discs.

Stevie knocked-out an easy-to-play
version of St. James infirmary
when he came to my house.
He told jokes, like the one about
the woman who dropped a bag
containing a dozen eggs and
a bottle of ketchup as she
came out of the supermarket,
causing a passer-by to shout,
This woman is having a miscarriage!

Steve's father was a psychoanalyst
of the Karen Horney School.
He kept a jar of cocaine in the
attic because Freud had done so.
He'd become a doctor in the army.
His pretty, less educated,
young wife brought textbooks
on psychoanalysis to bed in a
desperate bid to share his interests.

He was also a lefty, and he got Stevie
to buy the *Daily Worker* on his behalf,
as these were the McCarthy years.
He psychoanalysed Stevie, his own son,
and even got *me* in on the act
until I tired of watching him making
notes in silence, despite his intelligent
looks and his reassuring moustache.
The atmosphere became very tense
when his wife suspected he was
having an affair with a patient.

Steve and I became friendly with the
Hungarian wife of another Hornian analyst.
She flirted with us while we listened
to their prototype Hi-F, with its folded
Klipsch horn, which took up a
whole end of their sitting room.
Stevie's father told me that she and
her husband were insane, which confidence
I betrayed the next time I met her.
How the sparks must have flown
at the Karen Horney School that autumn!

His father stopped speaking to me
until Steve left for Academe College,
(hoping I would look after his boy).
But our friendship ended there.
I fell-in with the literati,
while he joined the volunteer fire-
brigade, mostly rich Yahoos
who found fulfilment racing along
country lanes in a red fire engine.

I felt guilty about dropping Stevie,
though we really dropped each other,
no longer having any common interests.
We barely acknowledged one-
another, across a mythical divide,
over the next few years at Academe...

We met for lunch on 42nd Street,
six years after we left college.
Steve's face had broadened,
so he no longer looked so weird.
I told him about my accidental
meeting with his father.
I'd seen a sign advertising
a professional apartment
on the upper West Side
and rang the bell to be startled
when his father opened the door.
He looked at me with pure hatred
and told me I'd interrupted a session
for reasons I was not conscious of,
refusing to accept any explanation.

Stevie toyed with the keys of his
new Saab sports car over lunch.
We didn't talk about the old days
as the years of mutual indifference
had made this awkward.
I'd acquired a wife and three kids.
He was about to qualify as a doctor.
He seemed calm and confident.
I doubted my mother would have thought
he looked like a cockroach any longer.

How sweet it is! 07.08.49

I worked in Mr Kaplan's candy store
for a week, when I was thirteen.
Standing on the other side
of the counter in the sweet
cold air hovering above the tubs
of ice cream felt strange and exotic.
I needed almost no instruction,
having watched Kaplan put-together
all sorts of sundaes splits sodas
and shakes innumerable times.
In making an ice-cream soda,
the trick is to shield the ice cream
from the torrent of seltzer with a spoon,
to stop ice forming around it.
But the egg cream reigned supreme
in the watering holes of the Bronx,
though, (as everybody knows),
it contains neither egg nor cream.

Kaplan left me in charge of the store
when he went home for lunch.
He'd empty the cash register,
leaving me a cigar box full of change.
I bought my lunch every day
with quarters stolen from the box.
Did he seem suspicious when he
counted it afterwards,
or did I imagine he was?
He never said a thing.
Maybe he expected employees

to have a finger in the till,
the depression having ended
less than ten years before.
I ate my pastrami sandwich
and fries, like a thief, in a
delicatessen up the road.

Mr Kaplan would let the kids help
themselves to comics over a soda.
Captain Marvel topped my list.
Kaplan shocked me just before my
fourteenth birthday, by asking,
wasn't I too old to be reading comics?
Smarting with shame and resentment,
I switched to Nietzsche that same evening,
but Nietzsche wasn't as interesting.
The Birth of Tragedy was congenial
to the spirit of adolescence, though.

Back as a customer again, at the
end of a hot New York summer,
I asked Mr Kaplan for a glass
of water after finishing my sundae.
He said he couldn't understand
why people always wanted to wash-
away the taste of their ice cream.
I couldn't think of an answer
but I thought of one the other day:
that you can get as fed-up with
sweetness as with anything else.
I seem to have made it last fifty years.
As Jackie Gleason used to say,
How sweet it is! Shazam and amen.

Romeo's spaghetti house 07.16.49

We arranged to meet at *Romeo's*
Spaghetti House, on Forty-Second
Street, just off Times Square.
It was actually called *Romero's*,
but I remember it as *Romeo's* because
it was the setting of my first date.
The July afternoon was hot and sticky
and the sun highlighted exhaust
fumes hovering above the traffic.
Wearing a white sharkskin suit
drip-dry shirt and knitted tie,
I watched the cooks fishing
spaghetti out of giant vats,
while I waited for her.

I knew her from school, though
she'd recently moved to Queens.
This was why we were meeting
in Times Square, midway between
the Bronx and Queens - not as the
crow flies but as the subway runs.
That week I'd often thought about
being within fondling distance of her
in the liberating darkness of a cinema.

I checked my watch about
once a minute, while a procession
of pasta dishes went past me.
I gave her another fifteen minutes,
forty-five in all, before I left, crestfallen.

When I phoned her that evening,
she said she'd turned-up an hour late.
We never met again and what
might have happened was left
to my thirteen-year-old imagination.

Two years later, I answered the
phone to a bunch of giggling girls,
who seemed to be calling
every boy they knew.
I recognised her voice, but
I hung-up on her, wondering, all the same,
what adventure might have followed
had I waited another fifteen minutes.

Yeast 07.22.49

I used to put in a lot of time
locked in the basement toilet
of my father's East Bronx bakery.
Today, the same yeasty
odour as that cellar's
came drifting out of
a patisserie in the marketplace
of a town off the coast of Brittany.

This rancid smell held
a constellation of sexual
feelings for me: the girls
I never dared approach
but whom I imagined
myself making love to
- not even that - just touching
their bodies - not even that -
only running my fingers
under their clothing and
over their underwear.

Their imagined breath,
the female form,
the very word *she*, set-off
my hair-triggered desire,
which, kindled by the damp
doughy basement air,
delivered me from the flames.

Death Valley 09.18.49

My brother retired to the
bedroom with his girlfriend,
leaving me with her
apartment-mate.
She was a fleshy redhead
with watery blue eyes,
liberally freckled and Catholic.
She was also a good
five years older than I.
Conversation wasn't easy,
as we hadn't much in common.

Her dressing gown
fell open above her thighs
as she adjusted her
position on the couch.
I made her laugh
when I likened
parts of her anatomy to
a map of the United States.
She giggled when I
cupped my hands around
the Rocky Mountains.
Then I slid my palms over the
Great Plains of her solar plexus,
finally slipping tentatively
towards Death Valley.

She didn't let me get to Death Valley.
I backtracked to the Alleghenies,

re-crossed the Mississippi,
only to crash again
within sight of the Pacific.
So much for my improvised game.

Then, we just sat and waited
until Charlie and his girl
emerged from the steamy bedroom,
she, radiant, he, shagged-out...

Driving over the Triborough Bridge,
he asked me what happened
with the redhead. I said,
Nothing much.

Paperweight City 10.13.49

The IRT rattled past the Yankee Stadium
before diving underground
towards Forty-Second Street - not far
from your old man's bar. What a dive!
(You and he were almost strangers.)
We passed a couple of matronly
B-girls at the bar, where your father
gave us rolls of nickels and dimes.
He was thin and dissolute; I could
see why your mother had divorced him.

We plied the machines with the money
at a nearby penny-arcade,
racing cars, shooting bears and
knocking-out plug-chinned boxers.
Then we went to see your uncle, the comedian.
He was doing a turn at the Paramount.
(Years later, I discovered his brand of sleazy
humour was prototype Lenny Bruce.)
He took us backstage, where I was
awed to see so many cases of whisky
piled high in his cavernous dressing room.
A powdered blonde and a seething brunette
hung around, waiting to do his bidding...

After the show, we joined the crowd
outside the movie theater next door.
Everyone was looking up at Dean Martin
and Jerry Lewis, poking their heads
out of a third-story window.

The hottest new act on TV, certainly
earning millions, but here they were,
entertaining the crowd for the fun of it:
blowing kisses and throwing down
confetti that swirled like snow
around a paperweight city.

II

Saturday night girl

Charlie at the tropicana 03.21.50

The Tropicana Bar
near Hunt's Point in the Bronx
on a balmy spring afternoon:
I was almost fourteen;
Charlie was twenty-four.
He slapped down a wad
of twenties and bought
a round for everyone,
including the bartenders.

(Whisky was anathema
to Charlie, turning him into
a Thirties movie gangster
by the second shot.)
In a flash, my brother
metamorphosed from Willie Loman
into Edward G. Robinson.
As this was not unlike
the usual convivial Charlie,
no one seemed to notice.

The whiskies kept coming up
as fast as he could down them.
With a beatific snarl
smeared across his face,
Charlie declared he was
all things to all men,
to all who would listen.
Little Caesar.
And he believed it.

The bartenders began
to look nervous as
Charlie's charm fell away.
He seemed to be declaiming
from some imaginary height,
revealing a man wrestling
with his own unimportance.

I felt for my brother,
ranting, piteously,
beneath fake tropical fruit
and stuffed parrots perched
on plastic palm trees
- yet I also *understood.*

Refused another drink.
we left, vowing to give
that Puerto Rican dive a miss,
the next time we drove
down Southern Boulevard.

Sugar 01.17.51

Helen and Jerry brought
Duane and Flo to New York
for the winter that year.
Duane could not stop observing
how *dirty* New York was.
A gulf widened between us
as he went on trashing
the city of my birth.
Though also a country boy,
my brother-in-law,
Jerry, was far more
open-minded than Duane.

My brother Charlie took us
to the *Metropolitan Opera*,
that is, to the burlesque
house exiled to
Union City, New Jersey,
some years before.
Leering comedians
performed their vulgar acts,
with obscene gestures,
among over-sized strippers,
bumping and grinding
to a bass drum beat.

Duane complained
he couldn't lose his erection,
declaring it to be
a *piss-hardon* - an expression

I hadn’t heard before,
(nor have I since).

The following day,
Duane took Flo shopping,
while Charlie, Jerry and I
went down to the Village,
where we were propositioned
by a pretty transvestite,
called Johnnie, in the back
room of a coffee shop.
His charm was undeniable,
and we all agreed we wished
Johnnie had been a girl.

The night before they left,
we brought the record-
player into the kitchen,
and brother Nick and I
took turns dancing with
Duane’s wife, Flo.
She danced very closely
and she French-kissed.

The surprise of it sealed
my memory of Johnny Mercer's
classy lyric, *My Sugar Is So Refined,*
which was sweeter than the smell of
my father's fabulous nut cake,
seeping into the kitchen
from his bakery in the back
- Flo's body moving
in ever-decreasing-circles...

Hat pin 04.18.50

I was in the first car
of an IRT subway train,
somewhere south of 86th Street.
A girl of about my age
was pressed up against
the front window.

I can't remember
what she looked like,
or what she was wearing.
But I do remember
something about her eyes,
when she turned around,
and those cheekbones,
and the way she
was pressed up
against the window.

Should I speak to her?
Should I stand next to her
- as though I also liked to stare
at the darkness between stations -
not uttering a word
until an opportunity arose?

I decided to approach her
and see what would happen.
She must have caught my
reflection in the window,
because she spun around,

menacing me with a large hat pin
before I could open my mouth.
She was smiling maniacally,
as if she'd expected this,
even *wanted* it to happen.

I asked, *Why the hat pin?*
She told me her mother had
given her strict instructions to use it,
should any male approach.
She said this without
lowering the hat pin,
or softening her homocidal grin.

Pretty girl. Pity her mother
had convinced her
the whole world
was a murderous threat,
those many years ago.

11.12.07

Mt vernon 04.12.51

I developed the strangest limp,
my left foot forming
eccentric elliptical loops
with every step I took.
My temperature rose to a
steady one-hundred-and-two.
I was also doubled-up
with stomach ulcers.
After the doctors failed
to come up with a diagnosis,
I was admitted to the public
ward of Mt Vernon hospital,
where I languished for months.

My nocturnal life-style must
have contributed to my condition.
I walked around the precincts
of Mt Vernon in the middle
of the night and was often
stopped and questioned by the
police, suspicious of a sixteen-
year-old night wanderer.
That I was on amphetamines
and in the habit of staying-
up for three days at a time,
didn't help either, (nor did my
reading matter: Poe, Dinesen's
Seven Gothic Tales and Nietzsche).
The biochemistry of adolescence
had done its worst, adding to

the stress of my trying to socialise
with girls at Seven Arts High.

I nearly left that elite
high school for the male-only
plebeian DeWitt Clinton
because of this.
I got very sick instead.
But there was another reason.
Our house was built over a vast
brick bakers' oven - rather,
the oven was an integral part of it.
Carbon monoxide, given-off
by the coal that burned twenty-four
hours a day, seeped into my bedroom
and into my bloodstream, bringing-on
a baffling series of bizarre symptoms.
I suppose carbon monoxide poisoning
often went undiagnosed at that time.
Ironically, I tended to discount,
even ridicule, my mother's theory,
that the house was to blame for
my illness, but which in retrospect
turned out to be the correct one.
It's taken me half-a-century to deduce this.

Just before going into hospital,
I attended a Greek Orthodox
Good Friday service, called
the *epitaphio*, where Christ's coffin,
lushly blanketed in red carnations,
is carried out into the churchyard

and around the church three times.
I envied the priest, (whose name was
Nikos Papanikos), his charisma,
which emanated from him at all times
- not unusual for an Orthodox cleric.
(If only you could bottle the stuff.)
I wanted to slip inside that coffin
while Papanikos was swinging
an incense burner over it.

He tried to help me,
to intervene on a spiritual level,
as had an American Hindu guru.
A follower of that guru drove me to
meet him in Greenwich Village in a
strange new car called a Beetle.
Both priest and guru were at a loss,
so the hospital became a last resort.
I shared a room with three men:
a plumber with lead poisoning,
an Irish-American company-type
and a retired German architect.
The plumber kept getting-up
to vomit into a sink by his bed
and he died in agony the next day.

The Irish executive didn't appear
to be in such bad shape and
we chatted casually over the week.
But the curtains closed around
his bed when a priest came
to hear his last confession and

to give him extreme unction.
I could not avoid hearing the
man's confessions of adultery,
of his fathering unacknowledged
children, among other *sins.*
He seemed relieved
to be unburdening himself.
His dying was a real shock.
It had all been too much
for this unworldly fifteen-year-old.

I turned to an old German
architect for company.
He was all charm and spirit
and the epitome of wisdom;
alone in the world and, no doubt,
aware he was nearing the end.
(After I left the hospital,
I went back to visit him,
only to be told he'd also died.
A poignant feeling of loss
surprised me, which I eased
by going through the ritual
of buying him a chrysanthemum.
(He may have had no family left,
but he had at least one mourner.)
His receptiveness had been a light
which contrasted with the darkness
between myself and my father,
who'd never once visited me in
the six weeks I was in hospital,
though only a five-minute ride away.

My mother came by every day,
bearing *Lorna Doones* and
bottles of *Gerber's* pureed apricot
baby food, balm for the ulcers.
(I never considered the
significance of the baby food.)

Rebecca, Muriel and Luticia, of our
cell of revolutionary progressive
students, surprised me with a visit.
Luticia shattered the illusion that I was
being visited by the Three Graces
when she tossed a present at me
from the far end of my bed.
(What did I know of ambivalence?
I later discovered she fancied me.)
It was one of many moments when
I understood that real friendship
was an impossibility for me.

The doctors were bewildered.
They treated me for everything
they could think of, ranging from
infection to brain tumour to cancer.
On Easter Sunday, three learned
specialists turned-up, unannounced.
After some discussion in hushed
tones, among themselves,
about how remarkably developed
I was for my age, physically, one of
them proceeded to hammer a thick

.

hollow needle into my collar-bone
for a bone marrow sample
I was conscious of the symbolism of
this happening on Easter Sunday.

Weeks passed. They tried a mega-
course of antibiotics, washed down
with milk and cream for the ulcers,
these being pre-Zantac days,
but still no diagnosis. After that,
I witnessed the agonizing death,
by diabetes, of a man in the next ward,
who screamed for days, as parts
of his body were lopped-off.
My own plight began to seem trivial.

Then two seemingly inexperienced
Pilipino interns performed a ham fisted
biopsy of lymph glands from my
groin, under local anaesthetic.
Again, no diagnosis. Fearing
the treatment more than the illness,
I discharged myself from the hospital.
After a few very strange months,
when I lived on Welch's grape juice,
(Welch, of the John Birch Society,
- those right wing crazies of the 50's),
regularly falling into hypnogogic trances,
I was able to walk normally again.

Boxed lunches 07.12.51

Visiting day at Camp Woodland's colony
of the Little Red Schoolhouse in the Village
- a summer camp for children of the Left.
I was a 15-year-old counsellor and I got
the job by pretending to be 18 - the 5 o'clock
shadow and my portentous manner did the trick.

The camp director and I were tying-up
packed lunches for the visiting parents.
My plebeian robotic box-tying technique,
perfected in
my father's bakery,
knocking-out two boxes a minute,
showed-up the director's patrician
fumbling with the wayward string
- three of *mine* against one of *his* -
forcing me to slow down out of embarrassment.

Think of it: *I*, the genuine child of a worker,
fearful of revealing my working-class
dexterity to this aristocratic Communist!
The paradox unnerved me, the first of
many political lessons which taught me
left can mean right and right, left,
as in tying a boxed lunch.

Far rockaway 08.10.51

I remember it as a seaside postcard:
two Cycladic figures leaning back on
a boardwalk bench in Far Rockaway.
My bankrupted father,
and my mother, both of them
suddenly old and visibly worn-out.
His white hair and silver eyebrows
temper black eyes that used
to burn holes through photographs.
Impassive, in my mental snapshot,
they glare at the shutter,
over large bellies, in blank defeat.

We rented a dingy room for a week,
on a dead-end street behind the beach.
On the first day, I met the
last person I wanted to see,
a kid from school, called, Howard,
who passed his days playing bingo.
I begged my parents to let me go home
- only a long subway ride away -
but they wouldn't hear of it,
and threatened to cut short their own holiday.

So I stayed on to witness their doleful week,
the old sailor and his bride,
combing the beach,
in the aftermath of the storm,
for the remains of their days.

Leaning back into the disappearing sun,
they forced a half-smile for the camera,
as if to say, *So it came to pass…*

In the beginning 10.10.51

We were a set of left-wing kids
at Seven Arts High.
We called ourselves *progressive*,
this being a euphemism
for socialist in the McCarthy years.

Seven of us: 5 girls and 2 boys
- all Jewish, apart from me.
We met in the basement
at the home of one of the girls,
with the avowed purpose
of distributing dissident leaflets,
publishing a literary magazine
and blowing-up the White House.

We only got to do the magazine,
as none of us had the guts
to stand by a subway entrance,
handing out Commie propaganda
to counteract the home grown stuff.
The White House was safe,
as well, as blowing it up
resided in the realm of phantasy,
as did sex, (for the boys, at least).

So, we were content to write
and mimeograph poetry,
solemnly collated around
a ping-pong table,
each of us assembling one copy
of *Logos* magazine at a time…

Muriel married a lawyer,
and she may have lived happily
ever after, (at least I hope she did).
Ruth went on to become
a politico in Washington,
(moving well to the right).
Lenore and Jake became
renowned radicals in the 60's.
Paula prospered as
a totally committed artist.
(Suffering was her gift,
as it has been mine.)

Rebecca made an unhappy
society marriage.
(It would probably
have taken her a lifetime
to survive her father.)
I was mad in love,
but doomed to remain
an amusing object
of curiosity for her.

We may not have arisen
to actual terrorism, (perhaps
we were too thoughtful),
though the passion that
flowed among us
is as alive in me tonight,
as it was at the beginning,
when the word was *Logos*.

06.20.07

You're vile! 10.21.51

You brought a new novel to school
every day - which gave me pause to marvel -
delightful tall myopic blonde of fifteen.
We were casual friends because
I let no one near me in those days
- and I still give most a wide berth.
Talking to you was like
stroking a languid leopard.
We were among a select group
of students at Seven Arts High,
who met on a small politically enlightened
island in McCarthy's America.

We'd phone one-another
to clarify an assignment,
or to set-up a Saturday
trip to the Cloisters.
Once, my dear Greek mother,
who transformed simple
messages into cryptic oracles,
told me a girl called *Yo-Yo* had phoned.
Bearing in mind she pronounced
cabbage as *garbage*, I puzzled
for days until *Yo-Yo* phoned again,
who turned out to be you, Muriel,
inviting me to the Museum of
Modern Art on a Sunday afternoon.

This wasn't a date in the usual sense.
Your law student was waiting for

you to become old enough to marry him.
After the museum we had coffee and
cake on Madison Avenue.
With the image of *Guernica* still
branded across our eyes, you spoke of
your fiancé in glowing terms:
his fine sense of humour,
how well he played blues piano, etc…
I was dismayed by the formidable
intimacy you shared
- utterly beyond my experience.

Envy caused me to blurt out
my bravado claim that I could
bed you any time I wanted.
With a look of blanched recognition,
you told me I was vile,
as if stating a simple fact.
I took your judgement on board,
transporting it to the phosphorescent
recesses of my mind, where it
condensed into a defining moment.
Muriel, you'd handed me
a hat that fit all too well,
before you stalked away in anger.

Mired in grandiose self-pity,
I typed-out a manifesto, wherein
I triumphed in finding my place
among the lowest of men.
I handed it to you the following morning.
I wanted you to know I couldn't help

being so totally malevolent and arch
and to call attention to the fearful
passion that gripped me, fuelled by my
own humanity jostling with its opposite.

Epiphany 11.15.51

On a mid-November evening
on an elevated subway station
midway between east and west
between sunset and night
I sat on a bench with the vast city
spread before me like a theatrical scene
in which a tragedy is about to unfold.
I saw it in the frozen alizarin cusp
outlining black buildings
against an orange sky.
The old story of perfection
manufactured in the mind
yet ultimately unattainable.

I had come from the home
of a friend whom I wanted
to make more than a friend
but her mother intervened,
so that was the end of it.
Like a wandering Jew in rags,
I left the house of those anointed
schoolteachers and their daughters,
poisoned with the impossible
knowledge of relinquishment.

Then I climbed the stairs
to that high station
whose scaffolding rose
like the constructs of my mind
and sat down, overcome

with the hopelessness
of my very being,
which, at the moment,
coincided with the threadbare
nature of all phenomena.

Adele 12.08.51

Brother Charlie dropped by
as I was putting the finishing touches
on a poem about yet another
unattainable girl - my first actual date.

She was fourteen, this blonde
cello-playing Jewish girl, and I, fifteen.
I used my brother's draft card
to procure Brandy Alexanders
in a small bar in the East 70's,
which resembled a left bank cellar club
- even the waiters were French.

As we sat in the erotic darkness,
over a sputtering candle,
I couldn't have imagined this would be
our first and last evening together.

I took her home in a taxi,
and while we fumbled in the foyer,
I could sense her mother's eye
behind the spy-hole of her door.
Not daring to touch her breasts,
I felt Adele's young cellist fingers
tentatively stroking my balls.
Was this really happening?

Virtually floating up to 125th Street,
I caught the New Haven to Mt Vernon,
where I passed the night mired in desire.

The next day, at school, Adele told me
her mother had forbidden her to see me again
because I wasn't Jewish. Full stop.
I took it like a poet and wrote a short piece
about sitting on a park bench at night,
mourning the loss of the gorgeous Adele,
with a street lamp above me blinking in sympathy...

After Charlie read the poem, he said,
So you didn't make it with Adele?
When I was your age, I took out
a different girl every night of the week.
You stay home reading books.
Are you queer, or something?

I was not insulted as I knew
Charlie had only said this because I was
doing something he, himself, could not
do very well, which is: to write about it.

Eleanor 12.24.51

Eleanor helped me wrap my Christmas shopping.
She chose white tissue paper and red ribbon,
which seemed strikingly sophisticated.
I put the lurid *Woolworths* wrapping paper
I'd selected back on the counter and the
parameters of my taste had changed forever.

Afterwards we necked on a bench in
Central Park near West Eighty-ninth Street.
We were both fifteen. Her breathing
betrayed the brute power of her lust.
I was hopelessly inhibited,
(sex, for me, being a function of phantasy).
Touching her breasts,
I was short-circuited into near-
incapacitation - a strung-out
adolescent lost in 'fifties America.

She closed her beautiful black Jewish eyes
while the force of her desire
held us in its sway.
Because I could not meet the beast,
because I could not love,
though drunk on the ether of her breath
and paralysed by my own desire,
I opted-out, disappointing both of us.

The young were not meant to
consummate their passions at the time.
But she found her *bonheur* with her Italian

lover at Harvard two years later
and a sort of immortality,
when they died together riding his Vespa
on a Massachusetts highway.

Rebecca above the waist 02.24.52

We were sixteen-year-olds,
partying on Central Park West.
You were leaving on a scholarship
two years before the rest of us.
While the others listened to records
you led me to a bedroom
and offered yourself - only the top half -
to my unfettered adoration.

You thought the exercise would be
therapeutic, or so you said.
As I'd been dreaming about you for years,
a dose of the real thing - in this case,
half a dose - would do me good.
That was your reasoning, and I bought it.

There was a catch:
no touching below the waist.
You said your mad father worshipped you
like a Greek goddess and had warned
he expected you to act like one
- denying the promiscuity of those gods.
He'd threatened to turn you into an armless
Aphrodite, otherwise. But it was
my arms that were almost amputated.

We set to it in the billiard-cloth-lined
children's bedroom of our wealthy host,
in earshot of Dave Brubeck's dulcet tones.
I was a virgin, though you may not have been,

both sexually warped by puritanical
'fifties America in her crinoline skirts.
Half embarrassed animal, halfway to heaven,
I wouldn't have known where to begin,
even if you'd let me go further.

I left that room, sore-lipped and
swollen with pride.
                    Born again,
I confessed to all who would listen,
that I'd lied about being your lover,
and, converted by your physical body,
I joined your father in his martyrdom.

Daniel and miriam 06.15.52

Daniel took me for a spin
in his father's new Buick,
after I dropped by
his parents' house.
It was on the right
side of the tracks,
in Mt Vernon.
(We lived on the other side.)
We were both
barely sixteen,
though he already had
a learner's license.

His sister, Miriam,
was pirouetting
in the living room
when I arrived.
I hadn't seen either
of them in the 4 years
since we'd all moved
out of the Bronx.
Miriam had become
strikingly pretty,
though she'd also turned
into something of a jerk.
This did not surprise me.
I also knew her brother
had the makings of
a homicidal maniac.

She assumed a number
of balletic poses as we spoke,
acting condescending and aloof.
I wanted to ask her out,
but I didn't dare:
not only was she too young,
but I sensed
she would refuse,
being totally consumed
with self-love.
(I knew her parents
wouldn't hear of it, as well
- besides, we would have had
nothing to say to one-another.)
Daniel drove me
down to the Bronx,
where he side-swiped
another car on the
Cross Bronx Expressway.
The other driver
looked on in bewilderment,
as Daniel sped off,
instead of stopping
to exchange insurance details.
Then began a 15-minute-chase,
which Daniel seemed to enjoy,
while thoughts of death
and of sex with his sister
conjoined in my mind.

Surprisingly, he got away,
and a Richard Nixon sneer
spread across his Glen Ford face.

(At the time, Nixon
was a junior senator,
making his name
by framing Alger Hiss in a
Communist witch hunt trial...)

That night we met up with
a nerdy friend of Daniel's,
who tried to entice me
to go out on the town
with him that evening
by flourishing a handful
of dollar bills outside
the telephone booth
where I was making a call.
How desperate for company
he must have been,
trying buy friendship
with a few pathetic banknotes!

I never saw Daniel again,
though I sometimes thought about
his snotty little sister,
my partner in precocious
sexual experiments,
four years before.
Yes, she was almost beautiful,
almost a woman,
but she was rapidly turning
into a middle-class
nouveaux-riche bitch.
What a disappointment.

Stockings and high heels 05.23.53

She stumbled on high-heels,
her nylons bagging at
the ankles, as though
it was the first time
she'd worn either.
Dressed for
a college interview,
she seemed out-of-place
in the hallways of
Seven Arts High.

Her father had betrayed
the Rosenbergs, earning
him thirty years
in Alcatraz
in lieu of Hades.

A child transformed
into a pariah.

We spoke a little, as we
had from time to time,
but I could not dissociate
my own revulsion
over her father's deed
from the girl, herself,
as if shrinking
from a leper's kiss.
(I felt a hypocrite,
as I'd refused to join

the vigil on the night
before the Rosenbergs
were executed.)

She would have a
hard row to hoe.
A hate figure
for the left
and for the right,
living in fear of violence
from without
as well as from within.
At the door of
womanhood, but already
mauled by history,
she was carrying daddy's
enormous guilt
like an evil foetus.

In the knowledge
I had absolutely
no idea of the terror
lurking in her world,
she flashed me a great big
lip-sticked martyr's grin
before moving on,
unsteadily.

I had a hunch
she'd make it
in McCarthy's America.

Sandals in the surf 07.01.53

We found jobs at a Hell's Kitchen agency,
off a sleazy hallway that looked like Purgatory.
Not much pay, but the agent said the tips were good.
Unfortunately, he was not as good as his word.
The seafront hotel we found at the end
of a *Greyhound* bus ride from 42nd street
was a machine for the exploitation of its workers.

We were hired as room service waiters,
which meant we had to hang around
waiting for a phone to ring in another dingy hallway,
which so contrasted with the opulent lobby.

You and I were high school friends, attracted
to a job that promised summer by the sea.
You were serious and responsible, if a little reserved.
I often felt you were on the verge of revealing
a hidden aspect of yourself - but you never did.
Instead, we held each other at a comfortable distance.

We strolled along the surf in newly-bought.
sandals on our first evening in Atlantic City.
The water stretched them into
surreal shapes, which matched perfectly
our slippery hold on reality at that moment.

We reported for room service duty
the next morning, at some unholy hour,
then waited for the calls to come through.
They *didn't.* You got two and I got none.

This left only the basic pay - which was derisory.

I understood the misery in the eyes of the
old regulars, who worked for peanuts.
It was like uncovering an infestation of cockroaches
deep inside the Taj Mahal of Atlantic City
- except *we* were the vermin.
                                        The next day,
we were on a bus headed for New York,
disillusioned and defeated. I went back to
boring TV afternoons watching the Yankees,
haunting bookshops in the Village
and drinking half-and-halves in the
White Horse Tavern with the ghost of Dylan Thomas
and with the aid of my brother's draft card.

I phoned you a few weeks later, to find
you were helping your father install TV-aerials;
hard dangerous work, but the money was good.
When I thought of you, brown bagging it to work,
I had a vision of the original kibbutzim,
straightforward and incorruptible;
an angel on a Brooklyn rooftop.

I signed-up for a couple of courses at
the New School: poetry with Louis Simpson,
and short-story writing with a rabbinical
type who made us stuff our work with
endless details of a visceral sort.

Years later, I learned that poets are born *and* made,
and that writing demands you desist

from stretching your subject matter,
the way our sandals were distorted in the surf.

A ridiculously high note 07.18.53

Let me time-travel
to the top of a mountain,
high in the Catskills,
where I will enjoy the company
of a girl I barely know.

By day, you can see
(I forget how many)
counties from this point.
But it is night, and we sit,
legs dangling in a deserted
hotel swimming pool,
lit from its depths by rows of
preternatural green floodlights.
(An unlikely scene for
an unlikely couple,
who aren't really a couple.)

We trek back down the mountain
and I bring her to my bunk
in a children's camp,
where I have a summer job.
(I think about giving her a kiss,
but I am far too inexperienced
and far too uptight.)

I grab my guitar - that ultimate
weapon of seduction -
strike a chord and launch
into a song that begins on a

high falsetto note.
This evokes gales
of helpless laughter.
I lose my will to continue,
despite her apologies
- and so the evening ends.

If I could have time-travelled
forwards, my worldly-wise Self
might have advised me
to grab *her*, rather than the guitar.
Unfortunately, I can only time-travel
backwards, so no kiss found
those ready lips.

Seven years later, I met her in Paris,
with her agreeable husband, (another
former student of Seven Arts High).
He seemed to have WINNER
written all over him.
They'd spent a year in Scandinavia;
Denmark suited them well.

That they were a perfect match
only heightened my regret
over that night in the Catskills.
When I think she might have
wanted me to take her,
instead of breaking into a song
starting on that ridiculously high note...

Louis simpson 07.09.53

Those sweltering evenings
in your *New School* summer workshop…
I was just sixteen and writing
poems about Prometheus.

You were a curiosity to New York,
a Bahaman Jew living in the 18th century
- at least writing as though you lived in it -
when you weren't struggling with Cervantes
in the original at Columbia.

Georgian from your Oxford weave shirt
to your tightly woven lyrics, you threaded
every word into a glinting tapestry.
Your style was to elevate form above
the flawed reality of the warp,
which often meant cutting that
perfect line out of a poem's heart.

(We nursed a shared delusion
that people could be taught to write poetry,
but I've since learned otherwise.)

How the anthologists loved you!

Then, I imagine a moment
when you thought, *This poem is perfect*
- but I'm tired of writing such poems...
From then on, you were moved to make
imperfect Jewish poetry, which captured the

suffering of ages, and the laughter.

Your style had lost its precious gloss
when you read those new poems
about your grandparents' life in the Stetl
at a small south London pub, in the 70's.
The casual tone disguised the mastery.

To think, I'd almost killed you,
your new wife and unborn child,
driving you to Academe so recklessly
in Wrigley's souped-up Ford, back in '56!

At the 38th 07.27.53

The New York Times became
a scorecard for the Korean War.
There were maps on every front page,
demarcating each side's position
on that immutable 38th parallel,
as though it were a football game.
Chinese hordes pushed us
alarmingly to the south of it
and they began to seem unbeatable.
The accepted wisdom was that
large numbers of dead presented
no problem for the Chinese.

For me it was only a diversion
unfolding on the other side
of the world, whose main
interest lay in the possibility
that we were not invincible.
So, I began to read the papers.
Brother Nick subscribed to the
Manchester Guardian, which would
typically run a large photograph
of cows grazing *on the front page:*
right in the middle of the fucking war!

One Saturday morning
Nick sent me to the dairy,
next to the delicatessen
on Kingsbridge Road,
for the makings of breakfast.
(That a shop could subsist on

selling butter, cheese and eggs
alone, is hard to imagine now.)
I returned with enough
cholesterol to kill a regiment,
but the newly laid eggs, frying
in fresh butter were very tempting;
and who'd even *heard* of cholesterol?

My brothers Nick, Charlie and our
brother-in-law Everett, didn't hold
an egg-eating contest, exactly:
they pretended that eating
a dozen eggs for breakfast
was a perfectly normal thing to do.
They managed it through sheer bravado,
though they must have felt
they'd each swallowed a cannonball.

The war ended in a stalemate.
There had seemed to be no end to it.
They were at an impasse
after the loss of so many lives
and they were wary of its turning
into another First World War.
So they called it quits at the 38th.
Americans settling for a truce?
Americans, who could nuke
an enemy as soon as say *die,*
who could eat all those eggs and survive?

05.03.04

ee cummings 08.31.53

I encountered ee cummings on West Eighth Street
on a Saturday night, in the summer of Fifty-three.
I was seventeen. He looked to be in his sixties.

People were heading for the *San Remo* Bar or peering
in bookshop windows or buying the Sunday Times
or trying to score or freewheeling on the night air
or deploring America's galloping fascism
or trying to visualize Rothko with hard edges
or weighing the day job against writing the novel,
not to mention Cuban abortions, Joe McCarthy,
coffin-nails, and the big C.

cummings shot me a needy look,
signalling he was on the prowl.
The thought of encountering one
so exalted dismayed me, so I walked on.
But I still wondered what this man was about,
what he might have said to put me on which path,
had I been amenable to his advances.

ee cummings with an urgent searching face.
ee cummings trying to pick me up.

Compassion 09.16.53

The concept of compassion
eluded me entirely
until the age of sixteen,
amazingly.
I was travelling home on the
New Haven Railroad with
Arthur, a clarinettist
from Seven Arts High.
With one ticket between us,
he had to sit in the toilet
all the way to Mount Vernon
to outwit the ticket collector.

When we got to my house
he began to talk about his
ancient Jewish grandmother,
who lived with his family.
She was on her last legs.
Her body had given up,
yet she couldn't lose this
courageous will to survive.
On the verge of weeping,
he told me how she had
to claw the very turds out
of her anus with her fingers.

I was taken with the strength
of his feelings for her
and shocked by the insight
that I had never felt such
concern for any human being.

Bluebeard's castle 07.01.54

Almost my first time,
except I couldn't overcome
my aversion for the young
woman I hardly knew,
who was coming-on to me.
She was my age, just eighteen,
though she looked older,
with a top-heavy matronly body
out of a Marx Brothers movie.

I'd given her a lift home from
our last high-school party.
It was seven in the morning
and her parents were away.
We sat gazing at the
George Washington Bridge
through her bedroom window.
The traffic made little star-
bursts over the elegant
length of the bridge.
We sat in silence, as her
hungry eloquent eyes tried
to browbeat mine into submission.

Her lust unnerved me, and,
as she was very determined,
I was afraid of what she might do
if I failed to make a pass.
She was powerfully built
and with a will to match.

Her heavy-handedness
must have been driven
by the many rejections she may have
already suffered in her young life,
of which mine would only be the latest.

A few years later I might
have gotten it on with her,
obeying Zorba's injunction
against refusing a woman
offering her favours,
though I doubt it.
                    (I was whole,
united in heart mind and genitals.)
I didn't fancy her, and I
could not force myself to.
(I also lacked confidence,
having never done it before.)

She had the drive of a chess-master,
of a top tennis player,
but I stood my ground,
hoping she wouldn't
literally throw herself at me.

Getting out of that apartment was like
breaking out of Bluebeard's castle.

The carcassi method 08.18.54

After my father's business went bust again,
we moved into a godforsaken house
near an urban expressway, in a marginal
neighbourhood, on the outskirts of the Bronx.
It must have been built over a swamp,
the mosquitoes being more than plentiful
and acting very much at home, congregating
under the bedroom ceiling every night,
ready to attack when I turned out the light.

It was August, and what got me through
the summer was the promise of college
on the banks of the Hudson.
That, and the Carcassi Method
- a do-it-yourself classical guitar course.
The simple exercises filled our house
with a kind of amber light - not a light,
exactly, more a complex sensory aura.
When I stopped playing, the illusion of space
created by open strings vanished
and I was back in that miserable hovel.
At night, the mosquitoes and the humid heat
often tripped-off hypnogogic trances,
suspending me between sleep and wakefulness.

One night I heard a tremendous explosion.
Realising this wasn't a trance hallucination,
I dressed and went out to investigate.
A long-distance bus was embedded
in the slip road divide where it had crashed,

the driver probably having fallen asleep.
I was the first on the scene of the disaster.
My ghoulish curiosity goaded me on to the bus.

The passengers were in shock, some
suffering broken bones and lacerations.
Worst of all, the driver sat looking
with detachment at his exposed shinbone,
which was jutting-out at a crazy
angle from the rest of his leg.
I felt guilty because I couldn't
think of any way to help.
Instead, I just stared at them
like a reporter from the Daily News.
An ambulance arrived in minutes,
and I took my cue to step off the bus.

I stood in the eerie silence, guiltily
grateful that something had shocked
me out of my summer's trance.
Anyone who's ever got stuck into
the Carcassi method will know what I mean.

The first time 10.13.54

Laura was a year ahead of me at Academe.
She was small thin and sallow
and, I thought, strikingly beautiful,
with her oval Modigliani face.
She held her body with exceptional grace.
I first noticed her in high school,
standing in a corridor during
an intermission of Bach's Coffee Cantata.
We come from the country,
We come from the city,
We come from the High School
of the Seven Arts...
She assumed a balletic pose,
feet at right angles,
as much an icon of the
Fifties as Audrey Hepburn.
I fell for her from a distance.

Two years later we found each other
at the same college, and
soon afterwards, in the same bed.
Her parents ran a small
grocery store in Brooklyn.
Her brother was writing a
novel on their kitchen table after
everyone had gone to bed.
Laura was a dedicated artist
and she was working on a small
painting of a sumptuously fat
woman, her physiognomic opposite,

(especially when Laura wore
jeans with a blue work-shirt).

I pretended I wasn't a virgin and I
suspect she pretended the opposite.
She wore various garments
handed-down by an ex-boyfriend
- a red-flannel shirt being her favourite -
and she dropped hints about a romantic
summer spent with him in Maine.

When we undressed in my dorm-
room, I saw she had small breasts
and that her ribs stuck-out.
The dark bags under her eyes
lent a certain gravitas, but
her manner was somewhat childlike.

As soon as we got into bed,
I picked up the *New York Times,*
which I pored-over for a while
to cover my virginal ignorance.
Laura waited patiently for me
to put the paper down
and to get on with what
I thought I was supposed to do.
I relied on fictional accounts
of lovemaking for my guide.
There was one story in particular,
where the protagonist, overcome
with grief over his mother's recent
death by cancer, pummels his

partner mercilessly, as she
rises to meet him like a hillock
thrown up by an earthquake.

But the earth did not move for us.
It turned out to be an empty moment,
leaving Laura looking even more dejected.
I picked up the *Times* again,
trying to appear nonchalant,
to disguise my own disappointment.
I'd no idea we were meant to
enjoy each other's presence,
to share the magic of intimacy
with the undiscovered person
behind the one we barely knew.

Instead, I entertained morbid thoughts
of Laura and her sophisticated friend,
frolicking in a New England landscape.
She stared at the wall,
while I went back to the paper,
opening an article
about John Foster Dulles
setting-up the first pieces
of his domino theory, which would
topple so many into their graves
in Vietnam, a decade later.

Death or the devil? 03.07.55

I fell into a hypnogogic trance,
(where I was neither awake nor asleep),
which happened often at that time.
I was in bed in my college dorm
prefab called *The Barracks*.
It was my second semester. I was 18.
A top-hatted evil looking man
with a gaunt face, wearing black tails,
peered into my first story window.
He seemed to be waiting for me.
I recognised the Devil
- unmistakably - and I told people
about having seen the Devil
when the occasion arose.
Now I' m not so sure. Maybe he was Death.

I once saw Jung's *Wise Old Man*
while tripping with Ronnie Laing.
He looked to be dying, his face
whiter than ash, and breathing his last,
but it was only Ronnie having an
asthma attack. He managed to stop
wheezing and turned into a frog.

I spotted Christ in the New York subway.
I wasn't in a trance - just overwrought.
When I told my analyst about it,
after his wife had opened the door
to me in her beehive hairdo,
he ended my therapy abruptly.

Decades later, I spoke of this to an
expatriate American who'd also had visions.
He asked me what Christ looked like.
I couldn't say. I could not even remember
the clothes Christ was wearing and the face
I conjured-up was cribbed from Raphael.
Maybe he wasn't Christ, after all.

When I was nineteen and fallen
victim to Montezuma's Revenge,
with my temperature hovering around 107,
Homer appeared at the far end of
a Mexico City hotel room.
He stood by the door, as if waiting for
me to follow, and Christ knows I've tried.

Saturday night girl 03.22.55

I used to visit you on weekends,
after the long drive down US 9
and a week's anticipation.
I was between girls and so you
filled that void every Saturday night.
You, a freckled auburn-haired
lanky woman of twenty.

Your mother, who would be
called a single mother nowadays,
would melt away to leave us alone
in her small apartment in the Bronx.
A gifted social worker, she was
considerate, to say the least.
I'd take you straight to bed,
without evidence of any
real desire on your part.
Afterwards, I'd get dressed, and say,
See you next Saturday,
and leave - all within an hour.

After half a dozen Saturday nights
you said, *Aren't you*
ever going to take me out?
I might easily have done
what you'd asked, had I
been able to take on board
the slightest criticism.
My answer came in the form
of my contemptuous absence

the following Saturday and
every other Saturday afterwards.

It didn't make sense - and still doesn't.
You were so bright and desirable
- might I add, *interesting?*
I was at loose ends and
we even *liked* each other.
Yet when you wanted to be more
than a convenient oasis,
at the end of a long road, I baulked
and thought no more about you.

A year later I spotted you on the other
end of that highway, visiting Academe
- that campus of the lotus-eaters -
on the arm of a golden-boy.
I recognised him from high school,
an anointed medical student.
The two of you *went well* together
- at least you *seemed to* at a distance.
It took all of this for me to realise
that you, my Saturday night girl,
were someone I badly needed to know.
Of course, by then it was too late.

The night donnie johnson died 04.19.55

I can easily remember
the night Donnie Johnson died
because Einstein also died on
that same warm spring evening.

The Academe campus was in shock.
People couldn't stay put, so the
entire student body of two hundred
milled around late into the night,
exchanging insights into why Donnie
might have done it, in spite of all
his talent, money and good looks.
If you didn't know him well,
Donnie would be the last person, etc...

That he was a beautiful black man
living in a white milieu didn't help
- in fact, his skin was palest café au lait.
(His father had written the Liberian
national anthem, though Donnie
was reared in rural Oklahoma.)
Everyone knew him to be unhappy
because that's the first thing
he told you about himself,
but so were many other students.

As a dance student, he'd partnered
half the women dancers, in and
out of bed, and many erstwhile

widows mourned him that night,
with tear-stained faces.

Donnie shot himself in suspicious
circumstances. It was rumoured
he'd been playing Russian roulette
in the company of a painter
- a rather louche son-of-a-stockbroker.
(The painter enjoyed trawling in the
depths of his own and others' misery,
and his favourite catchphrase
might have been, *You may
think you've hit bottom, but
there's always further to fall.)*

(The painter had stolen Laura,
my first girl, the year before,
over the Christmas break, while
I was in Mexico, and I laughed
years later when he told me he'd
lived in mortal fear of my return.)
Jim Academe, the eponymous arm of the law,
investigated, but nothing came of it.

The synchronicity of the great physicist's
death with that of this man of twenty-one
was like the conjunction of two planets.
Each increased the gravity of the other,
exponentially, at that moment, for me
and there was also something eerie
about the man who'd formulated E=mc2,
himself rendered into energy.

Donnie and Einstein became two sides of the same human coin that night, neither aware of the other's demise.

Diaspora 15.16.55

At four in the afternoon
I woke up dreaming
I was poring over
a map of the Cyclades
- except all the islands had
the names of tube stations -
just the opposite of the artist,
Simon Patterson's *Tubemaps*,
which might name tube
stations after islands.

When I woke, I was studying
the outlines of Embankment,
which was really Poros
and for an awkward moment
I tried to reconcile the real
place with the false name.
It is typical of a Diaspora Greek
to reinvent the Greek *nous*
out of the endless Sibyl's leaves
of Hellenitude scattered everywhere.

In 1955, I organised the first
Annual Dionysian Dance at Academe,
which went on to become annual,
and was put on every year
- long after I left the place.
It was only Greek in name,
as the students wore bed sheet
Roman togas secured with safety pins.

A Greek woman, who turned up
wearing an authentic pleated skirt,
looked strangely out of place.

In the centre of the gym,
our makeshift temple,
an Indian student told fortunes
within a labyrinth of sheets,
like an oracle in the heart of a maze.
He was normally quite conventional,
even overly polite, in the context
of that raunchy college.
That night he was dressed like a
Maharajah, complete with turban.
When I went in to have my fortune told,
he thrust his tongue into my mouth.
I was too astonished to object,
so I simply walked away, speechless.

As ringleader of the evening,
I might have done something about it.
But I didn't, partly out of embarrassment,
partly because I was preoccupied
with Laura that night.
She had betrayed me, and the person
whom she betrayed me with,
(that louche son of a stockbroker),
dropped her, in turn,
so we found ourselves in my room,
drunk on vodka and Coke.

At least, we tried to get drunk,

only managing to get more depressed.
I remember swigging out of
a family-sized bottle,
blinded with maudlin tears,
trying to impose my reality on Laura.
(She'd have none of it,
preferring her own.)
I'd hoped to win her back by
blaming her for my own lost desire.

It ended with what college students
used to call a *grudge fuck.*
(They probably still do.)
She seemed traumatized.
I felt a right prick. It was all so ugly.
So, it was goodbye Eurydice,
as she disappeared down
the stairs of my college dorm,
preparing to slip out of the front door
and out of my life, stealthily.

Smoke over troy 06.12.55

When I asked
William Carlos Williams
to read at Academe,
I welcomed (and was fearful of)
the chance to meet the great poet.
Modesty beneficence
fundamental goodness
were qualities you felt
before the handsome old man
even spoke.
He asked to see my poetry,
but as I started to respond,
another poet, who taught there,
my go-between
in setting-up the reading,
grabbed his arm,
and led him away.
So Williams never got to discover me.

The go-between sang in his
gilded niche at Academe,
where he produced
some excellent poems.
No doubt he was a kindly man,
but he harboured a hidden jealousy
for talent among the undergraduates,
(the go-between, not Williams, that is),
as many university lecturers do.
A blind area of envy - what we call
a secret agenda, nowadays.

He'd done everything right in his life:
his studies, his marriage
to a viola-playing lovely,
his professional career, which took him
from where he'd gone to ground,
in his thirties and forties, teaching in
my offbeat college by the Hudson,
to an Ivy League professorship,
where he might have crossed paths
with Einstein on the quadrangle,
twenty years before.

But it was his venerable quarterly
that put him on the literary landscape.
He sometimes asked me to read
manuscripts submitted to that magazine.
(One story about a man who polished-
off a number of six-packs
while lying on a hammock,
in the suburbs, refuses to be forgotten.)

The poet was Jewish
- and very Humanist with it.
How he relished that line
of Homer's about the smell of spit-
roasted lamb rising above Troy!
But he was most partial
to the Old Testament.
Then, there was this Oedipal
thing many Jewish men,
in particular, share with Freud.

I kept my distance, while
most students adored him.
I mustn't forget to mention that
he was a compulsive punster.
Perhaps punning was his way
of avoiding slips-of-the-tongue
- only *he* would have known.
A striking image from one of his
poems comes to mind, namely,
that of *dancing mirrors* - an allusion to
the mirrors in a dancing studio.
Dancing mirrors. A pun,
and a very good one, I thought,
on hearing him read the poem.

All the same, I wish Ted Weiss
hadn't discouraged Williams
from engaging with me.
But these were pre-Berkeley pre-
Sorbonne days, when such contempt
for the student was not unusual.

04.15.03

Beatrice 08.11.55

An open-air concert on an August
evening in Washington Square,
the brassy music painting ochred-
pink stripes into the darkness
between the trees. Suddenly, *you*
- parted from your man -
waiting to leave for Europe.
We hardly knew each other and
I know I didn't fancy you, overweight
and not nearly lively enough.
Pretty, though, in a painterly way:
the round freckled face and faraway look.
We soon realized we were
trying to pick each other up.

As we moved closer in the semi-dark,
doubts about the other were lost
in the serendipity of the moment.
Then our fingers brushed,
and in no time we were kissing.
Pressing your breasts against me,
you captured my thigh between yours.
I was struck by those amazing hazel eyes,
surprised they hadn't registered before.
I touched you through the loose
clothing, while you opened
your legs ever so slightly.
I brought my hand under your skirt,
sliding it up the leg, until I discovered
there were no knickers.

This brought out the Puritan in me,
for a moment, paradoxically lending
an element of urgency to the evening.

We took a cab to a midtown apartment,
where you'd been given floor-space
by two friends from Jersey.
Then, we made love purposefully,
though with little feeling.
I was put-off by your amplitude,
somewhat, magnified by
the hard floor beneath you,
as you were by my failure
to turn the moment into an epiphany.
Our desire had evaporated,
and it all ended-up an anticlimax,
quite literally, for both of us.

You were gone when I woke up,
gazing up at your flat-mate:
an eighteen-year-old, blue-eyed blonde
with a crooked nose, wearing a
coarsely knit sackcloth dress,
who was about to hijack my future...

You left for Europe, where she and I
found you, three years later,
on the Via Amalfi.
You'd gone native, having grown
more corpulent and more cheerful..
I don't think you were bothered
about my marrying your friend,

though plainly irritated at being cast
in the role of earthy peasant
for the benefit of us American tourists.
We'd become irrelevant, if not repugnant
- yet, that evening in the square,
keeps floating back over an ocean of time.

In the 42nd street library 11.16.55

It is so insignificant
I can't say why
I remember it.
You told me how
you'd watched a note
inching across the desk
in your direction,
nudged along
by a young man
sitting opposite,
who caught your eye
when you picked it up.
The note invited you
to meet him outside,
by the library's entrance.

You smiled your *yes*,
so you met between
the two Greek columns.
You didn't say what
happened afterwards
and I assumed
your story was about
the inventive way
he'd contrived
to meet you
- the only means
possible in the
hushed circumstances.

As I was falling
mad sick in love
with you at the time,
what stood out
for me was your
so readily agreeing
to meet this stranger
in the first place.
Though there was no
particular harm in this,
it still said something
about your character.
Or did it?

So many years later,
I still catch myself
trying to imagine
what you did next.

Better than your girlfriend 04.12.56

You phoned from Jersey,
entreating me to come to you,
all the way from Manhattan.
(I needed no persuading.)
Your parents were out for the day,
so we would have the house to ourselves,
with the prospect of unhurried sex.

A pretty black woman
leaned out of a window
above the IND subway entrance
on Amsterdam Avenue
to ask if I was looking for a girl.
I said, thanks, but I was on my
way to see my girlfriend.
She answered, *I can fuck*
better than your girlfriend!
Thinking to myself, *I doubt it!*
I let it go at that, and walked
on through the turnstile
before putting out of my mind my
unthinking *yes* to your command.

By the George Washington Bridge,
I boarded a bus that
crawled through Ft. Lee,
and similar nondescript places,
before it stopped in Ridgewood.
Flushed with excitement,
you led me by the hand

through your parents'
comfortable middle-income home,
up carpeted stairs and into your room.

I undressed while you
went to find your diaphragm.
From the bathroom, you told me
how your mother had hit the ceiling
when she came across it,
hidden in a drawer.
Then, literally squealing with
anticipation, you invited me
between ample thighs,
continuing to yelp
all the time we made love.
I had not known of man
or woman enjoying
anything as much as you
enjoyed sex that afternoon.

Earlier this evening,
walking by the Serpentine,
(an artificial lake, made
by a king to please his queen),
I thought about that day
and of our incomparable
drive to continue ourselves.

Dirty dancing 06.04.56

What a dancer!
She met me
with an upward
thrust-of-the-groin
on every other step
of the slow foxtrot,
hands-on-ass and
hardly moving,
there, in the
Zabriski Mansion.
The others were dancing
in the same manner,
but *she* did it with
barbaric authority.
Nineteen and swathed
in silvery sackcloth,
she was ruled by
her calculating character.
The heart pleaded
for mercy, but the body
would not be deflected
from its practical purpose.
Though she was light years
beyond me, she dwelt
on my every syllable.
But, as we were dancing,
I wasn't talking.

The street where you live 07.14.56

My plan was to take photos
of Borscht-Belt summer tourists.
I got the idea from Charlie,
when I came across a strange
double-lensed camera
and a box of cheap plastic viewers,
he'd left behind in our mother's apartment.
There were shots of elderly couples stuffing
their faces, playing golf, doing the mambo...

Nineteen and with no job lined-up
for the summer, you were game to have a go.
So we bought twin stereo cameras
on Lexington and Forty-seventh Street
and took the dark Taconic Parkway
to the Catskills, in a souped-up
Forty-Six Ford convertible.
There we found a *kuchalein*,
a Jewish chalet in the Jewish Alps,
complete with cooking rings
- really a tar-papered love nest.
On our second day, I took a snapshot of you,
looking gorgeous in a shiny blue dress,
with your blue eyes and Hapsburg gold hair.

Though passably good at cold canvassing,
I didn't begin to bring in enough money.
The cameras also refused to work properly.
We were broke after playing at living
together for two weeks, and you were on a

Greyhound bus bound for New York before
I could take stock of what was happening.

I ordered a steak dinner in a glaring diner,
by way of compensation, because
I couldn't think of anything else to do;
(I certainly wasn't hungry).
The jukebox was playing *On The Street*
Where You Live and this melody fixed
the moment on my memory, surreally
linking it with the Blue-Plate Special.

After a death-defying drive back to the city,
I returned the defective cameras with feigned
indignation to embarrass the manager,
(who'd been reluctant to offer a refund),
exactly as brother Charlie had coached me.
Later that summer, a man who
hadn't received his prepaid photo,
spotted me in the 59th St. Columbus Circle station.
I put on a Puerto Rican accent and pretended
not to know him, but he wasn't fooled.
Fortunately, his friend convinced him otherwise.

Back at Academe, I saw you riding like a pampered
prize in a racing-green MG, chauffeured
by this nouveau-riche buttoned-down stereotype,
who looked like Edgar Allen Poe with constipation.
Now weren't you everything
that was wrong with the world?

Dog days 09.06.56

Abe, Marty and I
spent the day gambling.
I was on a winning streak.
We started off at a church carnival
in the Bronx, where Abe reckoned
the trickster was controlling the ball
that ran into numbered holes.
Yet, I won. Again and again.
We moved on to a giant pinwheel
and I carried on winning.
These were only quarters
but I was soon convinced
that fortune was smiling down on me.
We were asked to leave.
So we moved on to Marty's parents'
apartment, where we drank beer,
sitting on plastic-covered sofas.
The leaden atmosphere of that
apartment exactly mimicked
Marty's bleak view of life.

We'd been accustomed to the breezy
groves of Academe-on-Hudson
and meeting-up in the city,
(in what everyone at that college
called, *the outside world*),
was an alien experience.
Moving on to my parents' dingy
apartment, off Riverside Drive,
and picking-up a few more

six-packs along the way,
we sat down to a game of poker.

Uncannily, I won nearly every hand,
whether we played seven-card-stud,
or five-card-draw, or just cut the deck.
I cleaned them out in an hour.
As I gathered-in the last pot, Abe said,
This should buy you a whistle
for your first freighter
- an allusion to Onassis.
How *wrong* he was!
They were both compulsive gamblers.
Abe liked to bet on the horses,
while Marty's innate fatalism
drew him to the roulette wheel...

Three years later, passing through Paris
on his way to Monte Carlo,
Marty left me half of his money,
for safekeeping, (that is, to keep it
out of the casinos' hands),
until he needed it.
I received a desperate
telegram soon enough, though.

Unlike Marty, Abe was good
at shortening the odds.
When I came back to New York
for my mother's funeral in '69,
Abe reminded me he'd lent me
a hundred bucks three years before.

He took me to Aqueduct Racecourse,
his refuge from the tabloid,
where his editorial star was rising.
Abe studied the form and the animals.
Then he asked me for ten dollars.
By the third race he'd won back
the hundred, cancelling my debt.
Abe had a high regard for style.

Marty moved to London in the 70's.
He'd married a sensitive Dutch woman,
and they had an intelligent young son.
We didn't have much to say
when we bumped into one-another
on Hampstead Heath, where I
invited him to my reading at the
Institute of Contemporary Arts.
After the reading, he advised me
to simplify my writing.
I scoffed at the suggestion,
and gave him a hard look in return,
but now I know he was right.

Two years later, Maryanne and
I spent an intense afternoon,
with Marty and his wife,
in our *bijou,* (i.e., tiny), flat in Hampstead.
I sensed his luck was running out.
I last saw Marty and Abe
in a Greenwich Village cellar bar,
the following year.
Marty was dying of cancer, but he

laughed when Abe quipped, blackly,
At least you've got your health!

We three were as bad with women
as we were with money.
We might have married out of sheer
perversity - such was the mess
we'd made of our relationships.
Maybe literature had diminished our
sense of reality, instead of enhancing it.
Marty won an early death, and Abe,
his never-ending youth, while
I got by on the luck of fools
and the grace of women.
I guess we all did.

A nice young man 07.04.56

I took a summer job as a photographer
in an opulent *borscht circui*t hotel in the Catskills..
The owner's wife used to wave me to her table
and say*: You are a nice young man, young man.*

Herbie, a raffish Korean War army photographer,
who worked at another hotel, called, *The Pine*s,
would enlarge my photos after I *soupe*d them.
I would display my pictures of people
eating and dancing, the following morning,
for the hotel guests to buy.

It was the July 4th weekend
- the most important one of the season -
two days that could make or break the summer.
Charlie wanted to play at being a photographer,
so I lent him my Rolleiflex, and made do
with a newly bought Yashicaflex, instead.
Problem was, I didn't choose the right flash setting,
so absolutely everything I shot came out blank.
A disaster.
                    Brother Charlie, on the other hand,
did quite well with the Rolleiflex, at another hotel.
Interspersed with his photos of partying hotel guests,
were several rolls of pure pornography.
He had somehow managed to sweet-talk a waitress
into assuming a number of outrageous poses.
My mentor, Herbie, was amazed at what popped out
of his enlarger when he printed Charlie's negatives.

After the weekend, Charlie and I took a walk
in the surrounding countryside - I licking
my wounds over a small summer's fortune, lost.
We wandered into a children's summer camp,
where I was horrified to see Charlie nonchalantly
lifting a portable radio off of a ping-pong table,
where it had been left unattended
- an opportunistic crime, *par excellence*.

My brother had often basked in
my mother's sobriquet: *o kelftis*, the thief.
Yet here was proof that he'd actually *become* one!
Was Ronnie right when he posited
that the identification hardest to shake
is that derived through attribution?

It only takes a mother to say:
You are beautiful. You are ugly. You are a thief.
You are a nice young man, young man!

I hear you write! 08.12.56

Visiting Academe in the summer,
when the students were gone,
was a sartorial delight
- especially that August,
when Abe was working
as a night watchman.
He had to clock-in
at various checkpoints
throughout the night
and the rest of the day
was his, when we had
the college to ourselves.

Abe had become somewhat
proficient at pool.
He thrashed me nearly
every time we played
in the basement poolroom
next to the gym, where he
spent most of his time.
My memories are of
being behind the eight ball,
of Budweiser and of countryside
resembling the golden Rhineland,
a hundred years before.

James, (who would betray me,
a year later), was living nearby.
I remember encountering

Saul Bellow when I went
to pick him up one evening,
where James was working
on Bellow's new house.
I was sitting on the trunk of my
souped-up '46 Ford convertible,
legs dangling down the back seat,
swigging from a bottle
of New York State Champagne.

Bellow glared at me disapprovingly
from beneath a Yankees baseball cap.
I said, *I hear you write!*
Quick as a flash, he shot back,
I see you're drunk!

Marty 09.22.56

I used to read in the old
abandoned coach house at Academe.
I even kept books hidden
under broken floorboards.
One afternoon, on opening
Robert Lowell's The Mills
of the Kavanaughs, I heard
a shot crack in the field
outside and a bullet thwack
into the ceiling just above me,
showering the room with plaster-dust.

I spotted Marty taking aim
with his hunting rifle and,
(assuming he didn't realize
I was in the coachhouse),
I waved to call attention to myself.
But when he fired again,
I understood his intention
was to terrorize.
I was scared, yet fascinated
by this display of Marty's
hidden murderous part.

His old world manners
and his old world charm,
complimented by his intellect,
normally veiled the hubris
he carried with him everywhere.

That afternoon he must have
allowed his mind to go
wherever it wanted,
that is, over the edge of madness.
He pumped a dozen 30-30 rounds
through the window where
I was crouching, before
he ran out of ammunition.

Was this the same
Marty who'd held forth
on the future of science,
when we prowled around
the Village, passing a bottle
of sherry between us,
resuming an argument,
begun earlier that afternoon,
in his mother's Bronx apartment?

Some twenty-five-years later,
his wife phoned to tell me how
Marty had tried, and failed,
to ward off his burgeoning cancer.
He did this by taking
imaginary pot shots
at the secondaries,
which he visualized
as a pack of black wolves,
in his mind's eye.

That mad blue patch of crazy-quilt america 10.16.56

An incident at Yale in '56, after the game.
Strolling down main street New Haven on a football
Saturday night with you and my friend Marc,
who struck up a conversation with a townie
to enquire after hotels in blue New Haven.

Pity Marc couldn't resist pretending
he was a famous archaeologist because
that made the man mean enough to tip-off the cops.
We left him under the eyes of the hotel clerk
and took the elevator to the 7th floor.

We had a bad case of the birds and the bees.
Marilyn-like, you revealed
the grand design of race-continuance
while I hovered like a randy Rabelaisian
bee over your invitingness.

My future wife at 19, you had a Roman appetite
for love, and your capacity for ecstasy
must have strayed the other side of torture.
I collided with your end-of-the-world, when
the door exploded:
This is the Vice Squad.
Open the door or we'll break it down!

Three men took specimens from the sheets,
and charged us with *Licentious Carriage,*
(sex being illegal for under-21's in New Haven).

We were interrogated separately
at the City Jail like common felons.

You "admitted" all while I cowered
in denial before we were confronted...
(Laws so blue you hear of men arrested
for kissing the wife on a public beach,
in that mad blue patch of crazy-quilt America.)

England got rid of her Puritans, not because
of her intolerance, but because of theirs'.
Denied the blessings of their women,
these big men with small hearts
are born to violence out of violence.

At the court hearing the judge asked us
why we'd come to New Haven to *do it*,
before fining us two hundred dollars.

Vinaver 10.28.56

Lileth dropped me for a buttoned-
down *feignant* who drove her around
in a green sports car all that winter.
I consoled myself by murdering Bach
on the guitar with Boris, the son
of a popular tabloid shrink.
Vinaver buttonholed me
in the hallway one day,
and advised me to never give up
poetry because poetry stood
between myself and madness.
He was stitching together his first revue
and it became the envy of us all,
replete with sharply honed wit and
endless invention, the prototype of his
future Broadway and West End shows.
Envy also hid his genius from me.
Vinaver was in a hurry, knowing
he was destined to die young.
When he died, in his early thirties,
he bore a passing resemblance to
the broken Oscar Wilde,
in a long-boned Sephardic way.

As a teenager, Steven had seen
the second act of every show
worth seeing in New York.
He had to sneak in as he couldn't
afford a ticket, but he managed

to put this knowledge of the
theatre to good effect.
His father, who'd led a Hasidic
choir in Berlin before the war,
must have instilled in him a sense
of urgency, born of persecution.
He phoned home free-of-charge
every week, by placing a coded
person-to-person call to *Steven Fine*.
I envied him his social ease
as I was lacking in that department.

I didn't guess he was gay at first -
so many women were in love with him
- not even when his unlikely room mate
showered him with gifts.
I have a nagging memory of Steven,
complaining to anyone who would
listen, how this nerd of a student,
(his lover?) had reneged on a
promise to give him his hi-fi
- an exotic possession at the time.
Then there was his annoying habit
of asking for a lick of the ice cream cone
of any passer-by holding one.
I only realised when *Private Eye*
ran a small ad, in 1961, which read,
Steven Vinaver is a cocksucker.

Steven's death brought home the
grim truth that life might end
with mindless abruptness, even for
one mindful of his every living moment.

I remember a long poem he wrote
about his affair with an actress,
while still a teenager.
It had an image of a row of teacups
which summed-up this woman perfectly,
(as he'd once also encapsulated Academe's dandy
professor, Roger Bottomley, with the line,
Mr Bottomley, you are a gentleman and a prick).
The poem was masterful and ahead of its time.

Abe visited him on his deathbed and he
described to me the terrible metamorphosis
approaching death had visited on Steven.
It was both sad and tragic, as Vinaver
would have delighted in the new decade,
having had a hand in inventing it...

January 2008: an email arrives from
someone collecting data on Berlin refugees
in the years 1933 to 1945.
He tells me Steven's mother, Masha Kaleko,
is one of the most famous 20th century
German-Jewish writers - a Berlin Dorothy Parker,
and a hugely powerful poet to boot.
Her *Elegie for Steven* is a heart-breaker.
He also tells me Steven changed his name from
"Evjactar" to Steven on arrival in the US.
Thank you, Roderick Miller.

Marred 07.25.57

Her analyst used to say,
"Take the *'I'* out of *married*
and you get *marred.*"
I struggled to keep a straight face
when my secret friend,
Louise, confided this to me.

She had roomed in a residence
reserved for the virgins of Academe,
where a vigilant eye was maintained
for the marauding male.
Though something of a twit,
she was certainly a good person.
But I wouldn't have been caught dead
in her company, and only
saw her after I'd left that college,
and after she'd lost her virginity.

She visited me at a summer camp,
where I had passed myself off as
an Arts and Crafts counsellor.
(I kept a car nearby - strictly
verboten by the camp's directors.)
After I took a nosedive
between her legs in the back seat,
to be repelled by her malodorous cleft,
sent high by the summer heat,
I settled for a more conventional
mode of lovemaking.

We next met in her parents'
comfortable Brooklyn apartment.
Her small boned finely
chiselled salesman father,
gave me the up-and-down,
in wonderment, before
Louise and I retired to her room,
where she told me the bit about
taking the "I" out of married.

Though she was hot and willing,
I couldn't hang out with someone
who talked the way she did
- no matter how much I lusted after her.
So endeth our last evening together.

Paradise lost 05.24.57

The New York insurance company
gave me the same aptitude tests
I'd taken two weeks before for the
bakery driver's job in Poughkeepsie.
Cashiered out of Academe, I delivered
bread with my friend, Ronnie Davis,
before his San Francisco Mime days.
One of our customers was Mickey Spillane.
We had a long list plotted on a bewildering
route map, typically delivering one loaf
on half-a-gallon of cheap American gas,
doing our worst to destroy the environment,
though nobody thought about it at the time.

In between these two jobs, Ronnie
and I performed a comic Calypso routine
around the song *The Big Bamboo*,
whose ribald lyrics appealed
to a borscht circuit audience.
Then we took a turn waiting on tables.
He used to greet me with a Yiddish,
Julius! You a vaiter? as we
passed on the restaurant floor.
I got fired when I served a large party
French beans *after* their dessert...

The aptitude tests were a cinch and the
insurance company was wrongly
convinced I could add-up properly,
and that I also was unlikely

to commit some psychopathic act,
(wrong again). So they hired me.
I was in charge of the suspense account,
(whose sinister purpose still eludes me).

The contrast between that office
and the Hudson River Valley
I'd left behind was painful.
Its effect on the sensorium can
be measured only in negative terms:
windowless grey rooms off Forty-
Second and Fifth, a greenish
fluorescent glare passing for light,
air tainted by the copying machine,
every spoken syllable mediated by the
pervasive air-conditioner's toneless mantra.
In short, an ordinary office.
As for what I'd traded it for, check out
the Hudson River School of painters.

Recently booted out of college,
I was now manacled to this grey cube,
east of Eden, truly fallen, truly humbled.
I should have been glad of a job,
as most would have, but I wasn't.
The Irish-American office manager,
a jowly man, who
commuted from Connecticut,
made no great demands on me.

But I couldn't stop thinking about wandering
through woods down to the river,
head abuzz with birdsong, and the

promise of a midnight assignation
over a bottle of Cinzano Rosso with dinner.
(Cinzano Rosso? I was a mid-century
American who didn't know any better...)
Then, of course, there was the poetry.
I got my sums wrong on the suspense
account for three days running,
so they fired me after two weeks.
I was grateful for this small mercy.

Playing ball with uncle sam 09.13.57

Those were the days of the draft. Unlike Elvis,
I was well prepared for my army medical.
Armed with a letter from my ex-shrink
that reported a deep-seated neurosis;
(he'd previously told me I shouldn't
even *consider* driving a car),
I limped into the army induction center
on Whitehall Street, in the Wall Street
district of Manhattan, with the aid of a cane.
I had pain in my right foot, misdiagnosed
as arthritis and wore a shoe, cut open
to make room for the gauze dressing.
There was a rumour going around Academe
that taking 50 aspirins on the day
would guarantee your failing the physical,
so I did, unaware that doing so was
tantamount to attempting suicide.

Speaking of suicide, I'd not only stayed-up
the night before, but I passed the whole
of that night in lugubrious conversation
with the most depressing person I knew,
who was a dead-ringer for Abraham Lincoln.
He got me into the right frame-of-mind
to claim I was suicidal when I was
interviewed by an army shrink.
I was even prepared to say I was gay
to give them another reason to reject me.
Then there was the duodenal ulcer...

I got special treatment at the center,
apart from the bit where you're made to
bend-over and spread your cheeks.
The medic moved down the line,
peering into the anus of each man, in turn.

I confessed to everything I could think of
when I saw the army psychiatrist.
My need to be rejected by the army,
freeing me to leave for Europe
inspired me to play the part well.
Having journeyed from station-to-station,
to be scrutinized by different specialists,
I handed-in the examination reports
to a black sergeant by the exit.
I asked if he thought I'd be rejected.
He glanced at the notes and laughed.
He told me - to my joy - they'd take
basket cases before they took me.

As I came out of the subway on 145th St.
and Broadway, I noticed a dancing
black spot when I looked up at the sky.
I later deduced this was due to
my having taken all those aspirins,
which caused bleeding in the eye.
The spot is there to this day.
Luckily American aspirins are
half the size of European ones.
Otherwise I'd have bled to death.

I could barely hear the ball game

on my mother's TV because of a
loud shearing noise in my ears,
but my ignorance of the real danger
I was in kept me from panicking.
The army sent me a letter
saying they could do without me.
The following day, I sold my two
guitars and bought a ticket on a
Greek freighter bound for Piraeos...

Last night, and 43 years later,
I watched a live game between
the Yankees and the Mets,
which began at 1AM, London time,
on the bedroom black-and-white TV.
Jeter was playing shortstop instead of
Risuto, with Bernie Williams
standing-in for Mickey Mantle.
Otherwise, not a lot had changed,
except that I'd become a sick old animal
- glad to be here, all the same.

09.26.00

III

A moment out of time

Bon voyage 09.27.57

My father and I took a yellow cab
to Brooklyn, where I boarded
a Greek freighter for Piraeos.
The old sailor warned me to stick
to dry bread if the sea got rough
and to avoid drinking too much,
which was the only advice
he'd ever given me - perhaps
meant to make up for years
of silence in his mind.
I think he had his own agenda,
namely, to cast me adrift
with his cast-off self,
back to the father he'd escaped at 14.
It was a gesture and not entirely empty.
Eat bread. Don't drink. Don't return.

Passage 09.18.57

The voyage took twenty-two days.
I never bothered to ask
how long it was going to be.
The Queen Fredericka must
have passed us three times,
sailing to and from Piraeos
and I discovered I'd paid as much
for my ticket on the freighter
as I would have for the luxury liner.
The food gave out before the end
of the first week because the
purser split most of the provisions
money with the captain
- a traditional perk.
This meant *faki*, bean stew,
and toast, until we got to Genoa.
(Even so, the purser actually
accused me of buttering
my bread too liberally.)
I saw a sumptuous meal on the
captain's table when I went
to his cabin to complain and
almost passed-out with the
shock of my mutinous thoughts.
I shared a cabin with an
anxious Albanian who couldn't
wait to get laid in Naples.

There were only eight passengers
and a homesick crew on the ship,

most of whom hadn't seen
their families for over a year.
They conspired to slow the ship
down to twelve knots, adding
several days to the voyage,
calculating it would then arrive
on a weekend, allowing them
to spend a couple of days at home.
Were it to dock on a weekday,
they would have had to sail
after only a few hours.
Watching the crew paint the ship
continuously was my main
distraction, that and trying
to improve my Greek out of a book,
(all the while imagining how they
were living it up on the Queen Frederika).
A great poignancy built
up in my mind, after
so many days of only sun
sky moon clouds and sea.

My first sight of Europe
was the lights of Portugal.
The ship docked at Genoa, where
I set foot on European soil at last.
I walked around all afternoon,
bemused by the fresh fruits and
vegetables piled-high in outdoor
restaurants, not the platters
of pasta I'd expected.

Before the ship sailed, I bought
a cheap guitar to replace the *Martin,*
which I'd sold to pay for my passage.
When we set foot in Naples,
a couple of days later, the Albanian
accosted a longshoreman, and
lacking a single word of Italian,
he made fucking gestures with
his finger through a hole made
with his left index-finger and thumb.
The dockworker understood
and directed us to a brothel.

This was to be my first-ever
encounter with a prostitute.
We sat on a sofa, surrounded
by half-a-dozen half-dressed
women to choose from.
A muscular redhead in a bathing suit
positioned her crotch at eye-level.
Definitely not my type.
In fact, none of them appealed to me.
Then I caught sight of a beautiful
face, almost hidden from the rest,
probably deliberately, I thought.
A dead-ringer for Anna Magnani.
I went upstairs with her, but she didn't
seem pleased to have been chosen.
She complained continuously
of stomach ache all the while
we did it, which left me feeling
slightly guilty afterwards...

Weaving through the small
uninhabited islands on the last leg
of the journey to Piraeos was pure joy.
I had gone full circle,
to arrive at the port where my
father had washed dishes, at 14,
before he found work on a ship,
to escape from *his* father.

Next morning I had breakfast
with two English archaeologists
who were staying at my hotel.
Refusing to include me in on
their conversation, they went
to great pains to snub me.
How I hated their pompous
condescending manner,
the more so because I couldn't grasp
the reason for their snobbishness.
I'd also never understood before,
why my father didn't care
for the English - actually he
hated them with a passion.
It must have been those years
he played the vulnerable grease-
monkey in the engine rooms
of British freighters, where
he was probably treated like dirt.

*(Have you heard the one about
the Englishman with an inferiority complex,
who thinks he's the same as everybody else?)*

Daphni 09.24.57

I found digs in central Athens
among white buildings
resembling old bleached bones
scattered over oyster shells.
The other lodgers were
a colourful bunch, especially
the charismatic Orthodox priest,
possessed of that indomitable joy
so many Greek priests affect.
The landlady was a stately
blonde in her thirties.
She had a ten-year old son.
Her husband was at sea.

She surprised me one Sunday
by asking me to take her
to the wine festival at Daphni
- chaperoned by her son, of course.
After a bumpy bus-ride,
we got off by a hilly wood
dotted with casks of wine,
which could be sampled
on the price of the ticket.
I went for the syrupy Samos,
and spent the afternoon ogling
my landlady, who smiled back.
I sensed her loneliness, and I
wanted to respond to it,
but I lacked the guts
to try my luck with her.

Instead, I got purposefully drunk
in that Arcadian grove,
made my excuses and
got on the next bus back.
After a couple of miles, I changed
my mind about turning-in.

I got off when the bus stopped
in the middle of a wasteland
purgatory on the outskirts of Athens.
Bonfires smouldered in the night.
I bought souvlakia from a man who was
grilling them over coals on a pushcart.
If you're looking for a woman, he said,
s*he does it,* nodding towards
a rather unkempt unfortunate,
who seemed to be scavenging
through a pile of rags and bones.
Overweight, and still in her 30's,
she looked to have lived rough all her life.
I walked away guiltily.

Then, I came across a hole of a club
- definitely not a tourist trap.
A strikingly pale woman,
dressed in black leather,
with raven hair and eyes of anthracite,
stood in the doorway.
She introduced herself as an *artiste;*
in fact, she'd just finished
dancing in the cabaret club.
I was instantly aware
of her considerable charm.

This was to be my first, but not my last,
encounter with a Greek thespian type.
She gave the impression she
was the latest in a procession
going back to Dionysus.

We took a cab to my digs,
and tiptoed to my room
at the end of a creaky hallway.
She undressed to reveal a dancer's
body: lithe and slightly muscular.
She again reminded me she was
an *artiste*, not a whore,
when we climbed into bed.
Uninhibited and eager-to-please,
my *artiste* was a throwback
to those 18th century actresses who
doubled as hookers after the performance.
I knew the landlady could hear us,
as well as the priest and all the others,
as we acted-out the Kama Sutra,
though I was too drunk to care.

I gave her a $10 American Express cheque
when she left, just before dawn.
The entire household directed amused
knowing looks at me, over breakfast.
My landlady said she'd heard I had
a visitor during the night, with no
hint of a reproach in her voice,
though I imagined she looked disappointed.
Later on, the priest knocked on my door

and announced with characteristic
gusto, *There are two beautiful*
women here to see you.
The actress stood in the doorway,
together with a fat female friend.
American Express had refused the cheque.
So we went to Syntagma Square,
where I worried the manager with
my passport and the *artiste* got her money.

The orient express 10.18.57

The Orient Express struggled
over the mountains of northern
Greece, en route to France.
My compartment was crammed
with people, drinking
eating gesticulating and
sharing their plans for the future.
A tiny couple from Crete
were bound for Rio, via Paris,
where they planned
to open a dry cleaners
and begin a new life.
Seeking to make a point
to a fellow-passenger
about U.S. domination of
Greek foreign policy,
I was nearly lynched when
I likened Greece to a whore.
I'd meant it metaphorically,
forgetting I was not in some
rarefied academic setting,
but in the real world where
insults could end in death.
(Happily, Greece takes nothing
America does lying down, nowadays.)

I changed trains in Zagreb,
where a long red carpet
was laid out for Marshall Zhukov,
Hitler's fabled nemesis.

He was on his way
back to Moscow,
to be carpeted, himself,
and written out of Soviet history.
I was carried off the train
in Aix-Les-Bains,
with an acute ulcer attack,
exacerbated, no doubt, by
the prospect of an uncertain
penniless future in France.
I was driven to a splendid
old world sanatorium,
with double-doored rooms
to protect me from the world,
which may be why I had
come down with the ulcer attack
in the first place…

Back on the train the
following day, I became
excited with the prospect
of seeing Paris, at last.
The train ground to a halt fifty
kilometres from the capital,
when the electricity was cut-off
because of a general strike.
This event confirmed
the little I knew about France.
The power came back on
three hours later, and we
arrived in a city where
everything seemed strange

and utterly exotic, yet
where I felt I was exactly
where I wanted to be
for the first time in my life.

Café des poètes 10.23.57

On my first evening
in Paris, I tried to find
the *Café des Poètes*,
(the one in Cocteau's film,
Orphée), which of course
did not exist. This didn't
deter a number of people
from telling me how to find it.
To be fair, they might
have imagined I was just
looking for a café where
poets hung-out,
directing me to the café
of their phantasies.

I walked around
St Germain for an hour,
being sent one way
and then another
by *helpful* Parisians.
When someone finally
told me, *Ca n'existe pas,*
I was puzzled
- not yet aware
that Parisians used
this phrase to mean
they simply did not *recognise*
a particular address.

I didn't mind not

having found the café.
The dimly lit bars,
occluded with nostril-
searing café smoke,
the bookshops and
the intense students
with their mopeds
- all those ineffable
vestiges of Rome -
combined into a kind
of mental Byzantium.

I had walked into
an enchanted city,
where strangers directed
a young stranger
to the café of his dreams,
though it didn't exist,
and never had.

Death 10.26.57

I'd no sooner settled in student
digs then I came down with flu
of the deadly Hong Kong variety.
The epidemic had hit Paris with
the ferocity of a terrorist attack.
Unable to fend for myself,
I sought refuge in the American
Hospital in Neuilly, which took
in stray American students.
I shared a room with a newly
arrived Californian executive,
who ran the Paris office of
a U.S. computer company.
He told me his biggest
problem was that his staff
turned-up drunk every day,
as most of them took a few tots
of rum with their morning coffee.
France was a far stranger country
than the one I'd envisaged.
The people were either boozing
or eating sugary yogurt.
Our energetic male nurse,
who reminded me of David Niven,
told me to cover my *bijoux de famille*
when he made my bed.

I was out after a week and soon
discovered the cheapest restaurant
in Paris, called *L'Auberge*,

off the Place St. Michel,
where you could have a three-course
meal for 250 old francs
- 40 centimes in the new Euros.
There was a slightly dearer
student restaurant called *Les Balkans*
on the rue de la Huchette, where
most of the waiters were Bulgarian.
It's still there today.
Les Balkans served its own version
of *Stiphado*: beef and onion stew
heavily seasoned with rosemary.

A few doors down,
a Greek patisserie, or *zaharoplastio*,
baked *baklava* in the back.
The atmosphere was amiable;
the walls lined with Greek dessert wines.
It was a place to savour the late
afternoon with a plate of syrupy
pastry and a pot of mint tea.
Aware I was in the most
desirable city in the world,
I had absolutely no money,
and no prospect of earning any, legally...

Like most Americans, I ventured into
the American bookstore around
the corner, on the quay opposite
Notre Dame, called *The Mistral*.
It has since usurped the name
of that fabled bookshop of the

twenties, *Shakespeare and Company*.
I walked into that place for the first time
on a cold October evening,
and picked up a magazine called, *Death*,
under the gaze of the moribund owner,
who said, *From the moment*
you walked in, I could see
you were obsessed with Death...

St Michel 10.28.57

It was late October.
My first month in Paris.
I was stopped by
a satyr of a man,
in the mouth
of metro St. Michel.
I recognised Jean Cocteau
- or *thought* I did.
Whether or not
it *was* Jean Cocteau,
or just a dead-ringer,
I felt a special connection
with this person
of a sky-open face.
He asked me
if I was a musician,
adding he imagined I *was*,
going by the shape
of my ears.
I told him I was a poet.
He said, *Ah, that explains it,*
before melting
into the crowd.

Chandeliers 11.01.57

I can't remember how I met
the Jewish lady who took me
to see *Et Dieu...créa la femme,*
on the boulevard de Clichy,
near the place Pigalle,
when that film first opened.
I was just 21, she being in her 50's.
Perhaps she thought the sight of
Brigitte Bardot - so outrageously sexy -
would get me in the mood.
Only Emmanuelle Béart playing
the harmonica naked, while she danced,
sylph-like, thirty-five years later,
in *Manon des Sources,* could touch Bardot.

After the film, we walked back
to her apartment in the XVIIeme.
It was full of oversized chandeliers,
far too big for her small flat:
(past grandeur, wishful thinking,
or just a good buy at the *Marché aux Puces?*)
I understood she wanted me to play
Théo Sarapo to her Edith Piaf,
when her doleful eyes
settled on mine, imploringly.
Not my style at all, I thought.

Rehashing this encounter in my mind
reminds me of how unattractive
I must now appear to the younger ladies.

Older and uglier, as the saying goes,
but I won't dwell on it - not today –
self-pity being supremely repulsive.

Did you know Sarapo means
I love you in Greek as mispronounced
by Edith Piaf? Everybody must know that.

01.01.04

Brigitte-3-in-a-bed 11.10.57

I dropped-in on Brigitte, who was
living in a damp suburban studio.
She didn't have a phone - hardly
anyone I knew *did*, there being
an eight-year-wait to get one -
so I turned-up, unannounced.
Brigitte was putting up a friend
for the night, a blonde secretary,
as handsome as Brigitte was plain.
Not plug ugly, but almost.

(I confess, I didn't give much
thought to Brigitte's redoubtable
human qualities that evening.)
They teased me about my haircut,
no fashionable razor-cut,
which was *de rigueur* at the time,
but a cut-price scissor job.
I felt provoked, in both senses.
As they had to get up early for work,
the three of us hopped into her one bed,
with Brigitte lying in the middle.

I lusted after the blonde, all the while
Brigitte and I did it, as discretely
as making love is humanly possible.
Afterwards, I didn't have the guts
to ask the blonde if she wanted a go,
for fear of insulting Brigitte and
of the blonde's rejecting my offer.

So I fell asleep dwelling on the one
I didn't have, wondering if she
was having similar thoughts, while
Brigitte snored happily into my ear.

The bookmen 11.09.57

At the end of the evening
we got together in a *Bierstube,*
somewhere in Southwest Germany.
John was in his forties,
a southern gentleman manqué
- all charm and triumph in defeat.
He would begin his pitch with,
Hi! I'm John from Atlanta.
That afternoon John pissed
into my hotel room sink,
referring to this as
an old bookman's trick.

Lance came in after him.
He was a younger man,
from New Orleans.
He ought to have been the one
from Atlanta, as he was
a Clark Gable lookalike.
Lance set up midnight assignations
with chambermaids in hotels
all over Germany, leaving
John and me envious.

(I was desperate to get back to Paris,
fed up with selling books to GI's,
too bored or too dumb to refuse them.)
Lance and John were serious drinkers.
They assumed an *out-to-lunch*
look with their first bottle

of *Barbarossa Bach*,
and were soon beached
on an island of easy bonhomie
and unfounded optimism,
swapping stories of gratuitous sales
and hotel hallway seductions.

As I drank my peppermint tea,
Loman and Gable sent me
pitying looks from their island.
I thought, *What the hell,*
and ordered my first beer in months.
Five or six bottles later,
we picked up our sample bags
and drove down the slippery
road back to our hotel.

That hi-fi 01.01.58

I'll never quite forgive you,
James, for taking advantage
of the situation, to nail that
au pair across the hall, whom
I told you I had my eye on.
You promised not to lay a hand
on her when I lent you my room.
But you touched her more
profoundly than either of us realised.
So I felt almost absolved
over the small matter of
repaying you for the hi-fi
- the one you built from a kit in
your army barracks in Baumholder,
the asshole of Germany.

An English rotter stole the *Heathkit*
from my room a few weeks later.
I'd left him the key so he could have
a place to sleep while I was away.
He got the Hi Fi, and you the
droit de seigneur over the girl.
I have since thought twice before
surrendering a key to anyone.

If only my hunch, (that she
and I would become involved),
had turned out to be unfounded.
At twenty-two, a couple of
years can be a long time

- the time she and I were lovers.
I couldn't have imagined that
she'd find you irresistible,
though that must have been
more than obvious to anyone.

Burly son of a Hartford
insurance broker, you were the
kind of jock some girls go for.
Mind you, Monika wasn't
always *that* discriminating,
and she was not averse to
the odd brief encounter…

I barely knew you at Academe, but
I won't soon forget that oil-drum raft
we made and lost to the Hudson,
and my embarrassing encounter
with Saul Bellow, at his house,
when I came to pick you up.

That scene came back to me this morning
on reading a poem by Raymond Carver
about a friend from the past.
I found myself in that old-
but-not-forgotten-friend space,
so started to write about *you*.
Then the sound of a vacuum
cleaner broke the spell,
and drove me out of the house
to a French motorway cafeteria,
where I retrieved the feeling...

After college, we ended-up
in Europe at the same time:
you, in Germany, *learning to kill*,
as you put it, while I'd beaten the draft,
and found students' digs in Paris.

We spent the first week of 1958
in London, (my first time there).
You enthused about cybernetics
and geodesic domes, while
both of us enjoyed the company
of his complimentary opposite,
which is what we were.
We marvelled at the inscrutability
of the Chinese waiters in Soho; then,
in a theatre on Shaftesbury Avenue,
we failed to pick-up two Jewish sisters,
whose ghetto mentality was so unlike
the mindset of their American cousins.

In the British Museum, I was admiring
an antique telephone, thinking it to be
a display, when it rang, all of a sudden,
and a museum guard answered it!
On a day trip to Cambridge, I asked
to see an original Bach manuscript
in the Fitzwilliam Museum,
and was amazed when the precious
sheets in Bach's own hand
were passed on to me to hold...

The next time you came to Paris

you brought along the hi-fi,
(a rarity in France in those days,
when garishly-coloured
Mickey Mouse record players took
pride-of-place in music shop windows).
I was meant to pay for it when
I could, but I never did - then
the matter of the girl intervened.

That's when I foolishly
told you about the grey-eyed
beauty living in the *chambre*
de bonne, next to mine, about
whom I had plans, though
I'd barely said hello to her.
So I gave you the key
before I left for Germany.
My time with Monika,
the girl we shared, serially,
was contaminated...

A few years later, when I was
about to move my young family
from New York to London,
you phoned from California, tempting
me to come to Berkeley instead,
as it was all *happening* there.
I almost did. I even bought a map
and memorised the counties around
San Francisco. Then I thought again.

The double 03.13.58

I bought an international
airmail letter to answer yours,
arguing we were both
better off without the other.
I re-wrote the letter
in the morning,
contradicting myself,
and willed you to Paris,
setting wheels in motion
I would soon regret,
reckless desire overriding
my survival instincts.
Then I got to work
with the urgency of
the impatient bridegroom,
extracting payday deposits
for encyclopedias they'd
never use, from GIs,
before they spent their pay...

Two months later,
on the road to Paris,
I stopped for the night
in a hamlet near Frankfurt,
where I ventured into a GI bar.
The air was thick with
boot-polish perfume and beer.
I spotted a woman of about
your age across the bar
- your German permutation -

sensuously built, with blue eyes
and blonde hair exactly like yours.
Acting on impulse driven
by ordinary lust,
I bought her a drink.

She took my room number,
promising to come up as soon
as she could lose her boyfriend.
I waited in the room for your double
until she phoned to cancel.
Her man *wanted to make*
a night of it, she explained.

I reached Paris early the next day
and woke you in your hotel
in the rue St André des Arts.
After some small talk
about your crossing
on the US United States,
I took you, unceremoniously,
as if to complete the unfinished
evening with your German double.

Without a hint of affection,
you became the prostitute,
standing-in for yourself,
withholding something
infinitely precious and ineffable.

I understood I was no longer desired,
(as an unwelcome visitor is aware of this

the moment he walks into a room).
But I could not save myself.

My sense of deadly karma
proved to be prophetic
when I discovered a rival in Paris.
My ultimate role was to be your *bird-dog,*
who would deliver this rival to you
by inspiring him with jealousy.
What should have been our first
hour together became the last.

Marital advice 04.30.58

We scrounged-up
two witnesses just
before the wedding:
my team manager
and his floozy girlfriend.
She'd slept in her make-up,
and before we drove her
to the Munich registry office,
she daubed water on her eyes
to avoid making-up again.
She called this a *cat's bath.*

The boss was a Polish-Jewish
quasi-gangster, living the life
of Graham Greene's *Third Man*.
He'd advised me to do a runner,
as marriage was strictly
for the woman's benefit.

Your Hebrew name
intoned by the German
clerk, recalled the Shoah,
most disconcertingly.

Afterwards, my manager's
girlfriend, waxing sentimental,
advised me to rehearse
sweet nothings, to be uttered
with artful spontaneity,
on our wedding night.

Then, we walked around Schwabing,
jumping out of the way
of reckless streetcars,
almost out of control,
themselves almost extinct.

What were we thinking?

Positano 05.14.58

We drove to Positano
in the middle of May.
I left the car-boot open
while we followed a path
to our rented house above the sea.
Our luggage vanished in seconds.
I wouldn't have believed
the *brigandi* of the via Amalfi
could make suitcases
evaporate like ether,
despite their reputation!

Beatrice, our American friend,
had emigrated to Italy
three years before,
and had married a local,
twenty-five years her senior.
She'd brought us together,
inadvertently, the morning after
she and I had picked
each other up in the Village.
She'd brought me to your
summer rental apartment
on 57th Street, after a night on
the tiles, actually, on your floor.
I remember you, peering down
at me, as you left for work
the following morning,
as if examining the merchandise.

Her husband was known as
the mahogany man, because
he spent his days fishing,
and the sun had turned
his natural swarthiness
a deep ruddy brown.
When we told him about
the stolen suitcases,
he *made some enquiries,*
and returned with all of our
luggage within the hour.
Positano was all aquamarine,
white, azure blue and ultramarine.
Mornings were cold and beautiful.
We ate *Crema Bel Paese*
and *pannetone* for breakfast.
The view of town and sea
was too good to be believed.
Positano's film festival,
and its rich German patrons,
hadn't yet set up camp.

I spent mornings trying to devise
a system to beat the casinos
on a makeshift roulette wheel.
(I never hit on it - ha, ha!)
We went beachcombing in the
afternoon for Roman relics
- often pitched-up after a storm.
I sketched-out a poem about loss
and logic, wine and the sea,
but it was never accomplished.

We ate dinner on the terrace
of a cliff-side *pensione*.
You seemed detached
- possibly thinking about
your other man,
though I couldn't have
suspected that *then*.

Your emotions betrayed you,
with a flaring of the nostrils
in a vulnerable moment.
(When I conjure up your
Austrian-Jewish features,
the intelligent blue eyes,
the weak, and at the same time,
rapacious mouth, the crooked nose
and the frizzy yellow hair,
I envisage those nostrils.)

My money ran out after a month,
so there was nothing for it
but to retreat to Germany.
You must have decided
to cut loose, then and there,
as I was impractical and
had no plans for the future.
My rival, on the other hand,
had applied for teaching jobs
at various American colleges.
Not party to this knowledge,
I imagined us finding and
restoring *une petite ruine*
in France, to settle down in.

Before we left, the mahogany man,
who rented scooters for a living,
asked me to bring him back some
Bosch sparkplugs from Germany
when we returned to Positano.
Yet his expression told me he didn't
expect us to come back,
at least, not at the same time...
Only my primitive need to possess you,
my appalling need,
was keeping us together.
We drove north in glacial silence.

Hitler's Moustache 06.03.58

The boss at *Collier's* asked me
to show a new man the ropes.
This entailed my taking
him around the GI bases
and teaching him the pitch,
managing him, in exchange
for an over-ride on
everything he sold.

The young Swede sat
in the back, while we
drove to Nuremberg.
He was polite and neatly
dressed, in beige shirt,
beige jacket and beige trousers.
I remember him with a
Hitler moustache - though he
may not actually have had one.

I jammed on the brakes
when he ventured that
the Nazis had been right
to burn the Jews in ovens.
You and I exchanged
looks of disbelief.

I stopped in the next town, and
dragged his suitcase out of the trunk.
He got out, and, without
another word, we drove off.

Interruption 06.17.58

It was one of those hideous
German GI towns, no doubt,
parts of it picturesque and
steeped in history, (but, for me,
only an adjunct to a kasserne).
The hotel owner forbade us
to wash our clothes in the room.
You broke this rule as soon
as we unpacked, hanging your white
Marilyn panties stockings and bra
to drip over the small washbasin.

Then we drove to the army base,
and were waved through the checkpoint.
I parked the microbus, discretely,
as I was p*ersona non grata*
with the U.S. military: (the result
of being caught buying
2 ballpoint pens at a PX,
reserved for the army personnel
and strictly *verboten* to civilians).
I told you I'd be gone a couple
of hours, grabbed my encyclopedia
sales kit, and joined the hunt.

Finding the barracks deserted,
I returned within the hour.
As I tried the driver's door,
A GI jumped out of the back,
his clothes in a tangled state.

You followed, similarly dishevelled,
both of you blushing deeply.
While I did a did a double-take,
the handsome GI straightened his tie,
and walked away quickly,
as if he'd just remembered
an important appointment.
I must have chickened-out
of confronting you, for fear
of putting an end to everything.
So I said nothing - as if anything
could have been said!

Anyone could see the kind
of woman you were, but I denied this,
categorically, in my mind.
We'd been married a matter of weeks,
yet you now withheld yourself,
both in body and spirit.
You would impose a humiliating
silence, one minute, and then
accuse me of failing you, the next.
You'd anticipated sharing a literary life,
you said, not that of a salesman.
I'd been summoned to save you
from America, which I myself had left,
partly, to distance myself from you.

Now you begged to stay in Paris
while I knocked around in Germany.
I resisted, so we joined the heavy-
hearted trail from base to base.

You were walking well ahead of me,
on the way back to the hotel,
after a silent meal in town,
when a drunken GI darted
between us and groped you,
fleetingly, before running off.
Outraged, you asked me, wasn't I
going to do something about it?
I didn't. Back at the hotel, we found
the owner foaming at the mouth.
The little Nazi pointed to your
lingerie, dripping in our window,
and gave us until morning to check out.

I remember struggling with you
that night, as I had done so many
nights before, trying to force breath
into our doomed marriage,
even overlooking your dalliance
outside the Kaserne, that same evening.
You resisted and I tried in vain
to browbeat you into submission
with my primary infantile logic,
while you bided your time.

Only a woman 06.23.58

Back again to Positano, this time
with Bob and Linda in the back seat.
They were on a European honeymoon,
heralding another short-lived marriage.
We drove through the Alps
on our first night on the road.
I made a note of the spectacular sunrise,
hoping the memory would put me off
committing suicide some time in the future.

In rural Italy, an old man filled
the petrol tank well past overflowing,
to dispense the full amount of my petrol coupon.
It didn't occur to him to make up
the difference in cash, even though
the petrol was flowing around the car
in a potential pool of fire and death.

Later that morning, I ordered soup
in a café restaurant, and was served olive oil
and pasta in a bowl of hot water, instead
- after all the owner wanted to please,
even though they didn't actually have any soup.

In fact, we were on an ill-fated
double honeymoon, Max and Linda, Lileth and I.
My new wife had rejected me,
when we were married, (6 weeks before),
and I was finding life hard to bear.
Like a hound among foxes, a Greek among Jews,
I was an alienated *'gentile'*,

though unaware of this at the time.

We showed them around our Italian paradise,
until my money ran out after paying for
our share of all of those posh albergo dinners.
Max lent me some to finance a modest scam,
halfway back up the boot of Italy,
where I made a profit by cashing-in petrol coupons,
without actually buying any petrol.

Linda, who was from the Bronx, and who
could have stepped out of a 50's sitcom,
became angry when I refused to share
the proceeds with them, arguing they had
put up half the money for the coupons.
She claimed they had to buy gifts
for lots of relatives back in the States.
For my part, I was looking for money
to feed my new wife and myself.

The drive from Naples to the north
was an anxious one, no doubt,
heightened by my mad decision
to choose that moment to give up smoking
- rather, to fail in doing so -
leaving me sneaking furtive fags
in roadside petrol station toilets.

In Florence, I was reduced to pawning
my new German electric organ
at the Monte di Pietà, among the local women,
hocking pathetic skeins of yarn.

Lileth eyed Michelangelo's *David*
lasciviously, commenting that
only a woman could properly appreciate it.
She had good taste in Renaissance erotica,
all right, the woman I'd just married,
who turned out to be not a lot like Caesar's wife…

In New York, later that summer,
Max told me Lileth had refused him
for the reason that he'd known too many women.
My theory is that she didn't fancy him,
being less than rigorous in her choice
of men, as I had discovered.

Max asked Linda, now his ex-wife,
(who was on the phone), whether she'd
like to speak to me, knowing she wouldn't.
(Isn't envy often assuaged in this way?)
Max enjoyed his regained bachelor status
with his flatmate, who brought home female job
seekers from the flatmate's employment agency.
Max regaled me with detailed descriptions
of raunchy Rabelaisian afternoons, stretching
into evening, on the Upper West Side…

Five years later, Maggi - my second wife -
spent the night with him, purportedly
discussing our marital problems.
(I kept a gallon of *Gallo's* wine in the
fridge at all times, that summer.) Though she
denied any hanky-panky had taken place,
I think it almost certainly had - going by
his mysterious behaviour the next day.

Max came to my front door, asking
to speak to her, but refusing to enter the house.
He looked agitated, as if fearful
of what I might do to him.
(Maggi would not come to the door.)

I can forgive her now because she's dead.

(Written outside a café on the Serpentine,
opposite the *beach,* where Suzi
is skating with her new guy.)

Amexco 07.05.58

Our last week together was a
microcosm of our marriage.
Always ardent, always rebuffed,
I couldn't fathom why you'd come
all the way from America to claim me.
Suspicious, yet not suspecting
your agenda, (so covert, it defied
thinking about): I was to discover
my role in your life, as *vehicle*
- someone chosen to take you part
of the way to a destination where
I would no longer be required.

We ate at student restaurants
and spent evenings in left-bank cinemas.
Peter Yarrow, from Seven Arts High,
slept on our Paris hotel room floor,
before returning to America
and inventing *Peter Paul and Mary*.

A few mornings later, I woke to find
you and your American luggage gone.
This midnight-flit from matrimony
set-off a week-long-panic,
to deposit me like so much flotsam
by the door of American Express,
where I waited to pounce
when you came to check your mail.
It was the week Corso's *American
Express* hit the bookshops.

Like a famished ghost, a needy spirit,
I searched every young blonde's
face to single-out yours.
Hungry and humiliated, I lived
a waking dream of loss, each day,
until Amexco's doors shut on the
last five-dollar-a-day tourist
headed for his two-dollar dinner.

Had your mother poisoned your
regard for men, I wondered, when
she swopped your father for that
Galician printer, you so hated?
You were a player in a new game,
(an old game, rather, with new rules),
among a generation of women who'd
discovered the utter disposability of men.
I'd set myself up three times, to fall,
always with the same predictability;
another stupid bee to your honey pot.

Sarah dropped-in every day,
eyeing me pityingly,
and I soon worked-out she was
checking your mail along with her own.
I followed her home one evening
to surprise you over your ironing.
You shrank into the darkness
with a silent-movie scream,
denying me my confrontation,
(for fear of being murdered)?
Having found you, I could see
there was nothing to be done…

Some weeks later, I bumped into you
and your new man, by the Odéon,
both of you looking utterly terrified.
He wanted to have a civilized chat,
but I saw red and, reverting to
my Bronx childhood, I shoved him
on the shoulder once or twice, pathetically,
before walking away, foolish and defeated.
I'm sure this humiliation caused me
to make a few others suffer, since.

Sarah 07.12.58

The woman who reminded me of
another who reminded me of you,
was standing by the Serpentine.
She was framed in a tunnel of
weeping willows, her body silhouetted
in the low slanting sun which shone
through her gauzy Indian print dress
- a theatrical effect of backstage lighting
passing through a scrim curtain.
She seemed frozen in a green tapestry.

This brought to mind yet another woman,
silhouetted in my doorway,
more than twenty years before.
Though I'd never given her a second thought,
the sight of her body, revealed by
the sun behind her gauzy dress,
had captured my attention, it was
so outrageously provocative.

Eighteen years before that,
I was astonished to find *you*,
lying beckoningly on my bed,
when I walked into the hotel room.
It happened on our last day in Germany,
after a month of flogging books to GIs.
You hadn't made a sale, which was
a pity, as you so wanted to support
your impoverished artist in Paris.
You were my estranged wife's high school

friend back in Rutherford, New Jersey,
working for a pittance in the
Mistral bookshop by the Seine.

You had given Lileth sanctuary,
when she did a runner in the night
from our student hotel room.
I sensed your pity and your eyes told me
she was with you, so I followed my hunch
and went to look for Lileth at your place.
The sight of her brought me
to my senses and apart
from a chance meeting with her,
with her new lover in tow,
I saw no more of Lileth, except
for a ludicrous divorce appearance
in a Frankfurt court, seven months later.

You were also Jewish, with an
ample figure and raven hair and there
was kindness and passion in your eyes.
You passed the time of day talking
to the poets students and anglophone
tourists browsing in the *Mistral,*
between the occasional sale.

I was surprised when you asked
me to take you on as a roving
encyclopedia saleslady in Germany.
You were to do the married servicemen's
quarters, while the rest of the crew
and I hit the barracks.

I never guessed you had your eye on me
when I dropped into your hotel room
for a chat on our first evening in Verdun.
You gave me no indication. I was blind.

It's true; the best way to attract
a woman is to ignore her.
You waited until the last night
of the trip to make your move,
after the others had melted away.
We shared a double room
that night, to economise - at least,
that's what we *said* we were doing.

I went out to post some letters
and I returned to find you
lying on the bed, wearing a transparent
nightie and a beckoning smile.
You burst into tears the moment we got
down to it, calling yourself a whore.
I offered to stop, but you
told me to *go on and finish.*
I asked no more questions.
                                        Your painter
was twenty years older than you,
a concentration-camp survivor.

You planned to emigrate to Canada.
When you said you'd *have* to tell him
about our evening, I pointed-out this
wasn't strictly necessary - but you insisted.
It occurs to me, only now,

that you might have done it for
the guilt as much as for the sex.

A few weeks afterwards, my girlfriend, Monika,
and I dropped-in on you and your painter
in the rented house in Lagny-sur-Marne,
of French Impressionist fame.
(We lived in proletarian Gagny.)
His large grey paintings were mountains
of non-objective undifferentiated forms.
It was my first brush with Minimalism.
I thought the work ridiculous, though potent
and mysterious, at the same time,
and, I must admit I envied your painter.

It was obvious you'd confessed
to your indiscretion, as he
didn't look pleased to see me.
My dog was worrying his exotic African
fowl ranging free around the garden.
As I was giving him my assurances that
Biela, my black poodle, was harmless,
she sank her teeth into the bird.
I offered embarrassed apologies
and payment, (both refused),
before beating a hasty retreat.
This was to be the last time I saw you.

I heard you'd made it
to Canada, set-up a pottery,
even had a child, I think.
I believe I heard your painter died

soon afterwards - I'm not certain...

As I got up to leave the café where
I set down these lines, a woman
passed by in a translucent dress.
She must have been wearing a slip,
because, although the sun was behind her,
her body was nowhere to be seen.

05.13.00

Je suis un vrai 10.10.58

A young Berber wearing a
sheepskin coat leaned
against the zinc bar
of the *Cinq Billards*
on the Place de la Contrescarpe.
He kept repeating,
Je suis un vrai!
all the while
looking absolutely miserable.
(Was he implying
the rest of us weren't?)

His words have stuck
in my mind over the years.
Is it that nomads need to reassure
themselves of their identity,
frequently, having no home,
no familiar neighbourhood,
to do it for them, all places
being equally familiar?
Did he want to be contradicted
in order to spark-off
a cathartic exchange of views?
But, he wasn't satisfied
when I agreed with him and
he continued to repeat,
Je suis un vrai!

It was two in the morning.
The cafés of the Fourth Republic

were just coming to life.
Posters in the Metro exhorted
the public to drink no more
than one litre of wine a day.
One litre a day!
I was tipsy on white wine,
and his relentless repetition
of the words, *Je suis un vrai*,
began to irritate, so I left
to go on an extended café-crawl
across Paris, where these two lines
of poetry leached into my brain:
J'ai passé une nuit blanche
parmis des arbres de sable.
This image summed-up
my surreal state-of-mind.

I was feeling bereft and poor
by the time I got to the Madelaine.
I wished I had a father
to support me in Paris,
someone to underwrite my career.
He might own a furniture store
in the Boulevard des Italiens…
This may explain why I ended-up
in that most solid of businesses,
the piano game, where I have
become my father, in a way.
Je suis un vrai!

I would have liked her 09.11.58

He was a young American
living the *Lost Generation* dream.
He wrote short stories, though
his wife was sick with anxiety
because they had no money.
They lived near the rue St. Jacques
- a stone's throw from Notre Dame.

She wanted me to talk to him
about finding a job:
(embarrassing, as I hardly
knew either of them).
She said, as I seemed to be
making a decent living,
couldn't I give him a job,
or help him find one?
I tried a man-to-man
on the subject of gainful
employment, but he dismissed
my meddling with contempt.

I secretly envied him his *doing*
a Hemingway; not giving
a shit about what others
thought - not even his wife!
I knew they were nearly newlyweds,
but that didn't stop me from
thinking about offering myself
to her as an alternative to him.

She was Athene-eyed and beautiful,
fine-boned and brimming with *life.*
A patrician Jewess.
What was she doing with this loser?
Maybe she'd intuited I was one, too.
Perhaps not a loser, just a man
whose extraordinary industry tended
to produce disappointing outcomes.
But I guessed it wasn't in her
nature to be unfaithful, so I didn't try.
But I would have *liked* to.

Chez maurice 10.19.58

Chez Maurice was my refuge
from the day Lileth did a runner,
to the day Maurice refused me a short-
term loan of five-thousand old francs.
Located on a corner between the
Odeon and the Luxembourg Gardens,
it was frequented by a set of young
alcoholic down-and-outs, which
I joined - if only in spirit. (Ha ha.)

Among them, there was a fatalistic
Lebanese medical student
who literally drank himself to death,
Brigitte, a homely Belgian woman
with a healthy sexual appetite,
a soulful Frenchwoman in her
twenties who seemed to be
quietly suffering all the time,
a tall thin lost American from
the Midwest, who could out-
drink everyone around, except
his young freckled girlfriend.
(She'd come over from California
on the proceeds of her father's
US government insurance policy.
He'd been a nuclear physicist,
and had died in dark circumstances.)

And a few others… Maurice would make
crêpes for us when it wasn't busy.

He was a Breton, and like many
of his countrymen, he seemed to have
just stepped out of the Gare Montparnasse,
though he'd lived in Paris
for years and owned the café.
We all sat in the back room,
between the *flipper,* (pin-ball
machine), and the toilet, which was almost
close enough to expose us to splash back,
and the odour of piss and beer
was so pervasive, that the thought of
these brings the place back, vividly.

Paris was a city of haves and have-nots.
It was teeming with the disenfranchised,
for example: painters who couldn't
afford a studio, yet lived
in hope of unearthing a cheap one
and who talked about nothing else.
We sat around drinking beer
and trading tips about survival
in that ruthless city of the fifties,
just waking out of World War Two
and bursting with temptation.
The jukebox played the same
rock-and-roll record over and over
but nobody seemed to mind.

David, a dashing English ex-navy,
petty-criminal type, told a joke about
a couple who were having sex in the
garden of the woman's family home.

At the critical moment, just as the man
was about to withdraw, the woman's mother,
who had come out to look for them,
accidentally stepped on his derriere,
causing her daughter to become pregnant.
The presiding judge at the paternity
hearing, after much deliberation, determined
that the grandmother was the child's father.

One night, David confided he was planning
to cook a joint of lamb and he offered
to share it with me in my room the
following day, adding, he'd be obliged if
I'd provide a can of flageolets to go with it.
That same evening the nuclear physicist's
daughter asked me to put her up for the
night, because she'd had a violent
argument with her Midwesterner.
When David turned-up in the morning,
with his leg of lamb, he glared at her
rather soiled underwear, lying all
over the floor, and remarked that
a Frenchwoman wouldn't be caught
dead wearing such dirty knickers.
I gave David a job flogging books
to GIs, but it wasn't his cup of tea.
Some craven betrayal on his part
prompted me to call him a coward.
He said, no officer of Her Majesty's
Navy would allow himself be called a coward.
Later on, when he asked to borrow my room
while I was away for a couple of weeks,

I handed over the keys, reluctantly,
only to find it had been burgled, on my return...
Then Maurice refused me the small loan,
and I never went back to that café again.

Bridge rage 10.20.58

I must have cut him off
near the Châtelet end
of the Pont au Change,
for, when I stopped at
the lights, I was surprised
when the motorcyclist
thrust his hairy arm
through my car window
and grabbed me by the collar.
He was about thirty and
burley, and he expressed
his unbridled anger by
shaking me like a kitten
while he delivered
a cascade of epithets.

His fat face danced
before the background of the
Sarah Bernhardt Theatre,
(which was really my head
bobbing up and down).
We attracted an audience
of passers-by, fascinated
by the sight of a young
foreigner in an old *Hudson,*
with tourist plates, getting throttled.

By chance, a carpenter's hammer
was lying right beside me
on the passenger seat.

I considered hitting him with it,
for a moment, figuring if I
whacked him on the forearm
and drove-off quickly,
I might just get away.

Then again, I might have ended-up
smashing his head in, perhaps
leaving a family fatherless,
and myself imprisoned for life.
Or he might have become enraged
with the first blow of the hammer,
and done *me* some serious damage.
Grab the hammer, or leave it?
I couldn't decide, but the
fact of its being there
was a comfort of sorts,
so I tolerated his rage,
hoping, at the same time,
he wouldn't open the door.

He finally let go, with a
look of jowly satisfaction.
Then he pumped the starter
of his bike and roared off towards
the Boulevard Sébastopol.
It was the month of October,
in the middle of the afternoon,
and the sun heightened
the colours of the cafés and
theatres around the Châtelet.
There had been no massacre.

A fragonard 10.26.58

I met her at a party
near the Ecole Militaire,
though the circumstances
of our meeting are clouded
in the miasma of 40 years.
She walked right out of
a Fragonard painting:
the one of a girl perched,
provocatively, on a swing.
A veritable *Little Bo Peep*,
dressed for a thé dansante
in a florid peasant frock,
immaculately made-up,
with insouciant eyes,
(fetching, in a china
doll kind of a way).
Her manner was also
pleasant and unaffected.

As the party came to an end
she confided she was
new to Paris and had
nowhere to stay that night.
Could I put her up?
Hiding my eagerness,
I said, *Mi casa, su casa,*
and we headed for my place.
But when I tried to kiss
her at the lights on the
Ile de la Cité, she told me
she was a Lesbian.

Without hesitation,
I opened the car door
and told her to get out,
surprising myself
with my own anger.
This soon merged with
guilt over having so
callously left a vulnerable
young woman to her fate
in the middle of the night,
in what was, for her,
a strange city.

Afterwards, I thought,
I should have taken her home,
fixed her a drink,
found out what it was like
to be living her life,
(if she was willing to tell me).
I would have given her my bed,
while I took to the floor.
I really should have
- but that Lesbian bitch
was too beautiful.

Mahogany footstool 12.01.58

Florencie played flamenco guitar
in a dark left bank club.
His playing wasn't that accomplished,
but his aquiline features
more than made up for
any deficiencies of technique.
He reprised the same repertoire
every night, opening with
the soundtrack of *Forbidden Games*,
(which any beginner can play,
though without the benefit
of his pallid beauty),
and ending with Albaniz's *Esturias*.
(Alain Resnais gave him
a one-line walk-on role as
a barman in *Shoot The Pianist*.)
Adoring fans, mainly women,
came to hear him play the same
pieces, night after night, as I did.

One evening I asked him to
put me on to his teacher,
whom I found in a poor fifth-
floor tenement in Montmartre.
His heart condition preventing him
from playing in smoky nightclubs,
the teacher had passed on the torch
to his teenage daughter,
who now supported
the whole gypsy family,

including a beaming toddler.
He was very charismatic,
but his teaching methods
were rigorous in the extreme.
He believed every exercise
should strengthen the fingers,
so he deliberately chose athletic
fingerings to that end,
making progress maddeningly difficult.

I bought mahogany to make a footstool,
for use when playing the guitar.
But, the wood was so hard,
it defeated every drill I could find.
Struggling with the teacher's
inflexible method, and with
the footstool that didn't
want to come into being,
(remaining, instead,
a sort of Platonic ideal),
I finally gave up on both.
My dream of becoming
an *après souper* idol
in a cellar club evaporated...

One year later, in New York,
I plodded-through the Albaniz
for my guitarist friend, Max,
who then played it for me, effortlessly,
using simple logical fingerings.
I realised I'd been right
to drop the gypsy teacher.

But the footstool still haunted me.
It symbolised my tendency
to lose the plot, and I began
to fear my life was becoming an
endless series of fruitless byroads.

The chambre de bonne 12.06.58

An evening in a left-bank cellar club;
Florencie playing guitar in the darkness;
French cognac German women love so well.
And you were resolutely German, except
for that touch of the young Ingrid Bergman,
your Swedish name belying an Italian mother.

I was surprised at your tongue's answer
when my mouth put the question to your lips,
surprised especially as a G.I. friend
who'd borrowed my room, next to yours,
bedded you, though he'd promised not to try.

The grey industrial sackcloth dress
became a fetish in my imagination,
your breasts yielding under mineral cloth:
metallic drapery gathering
above marble-white thighs.

You slipped off sensible German knickers
to expose a dense Venusian thatch
beneath the steely headlands of your dress.
Then, throwing your head to one side,
you waited for your pleasure to discover you...

But, you wouldn't spend the night with me,
and I hadn't even seen you fully naked.
Some months after, you confessed
to having made love with me that evening,
only because my room reminded you
of *your* night with my friend.

A moment out of time 01.11.59

It was a moment out of time.
I was standing outside of
the *Maison de Café,*
biting into a moist
Salade Niçoise sandwich,
still half in its wrapper.
The morning traffic was
swirling around the Opéra.

For no apparent reason
I looked up at a small white
January sun, appearing and
disappearing through gauzy clouds.
It was like peering into a mirror
at a bleak witness to our days,
a false eclipse, the face
of indifference and of truth.

I was on my way to meet you.
We'd only known each other
for a couple of weeks.
We wanted to connect,
only we didn't really,
and were to spend
two years denying it.
At that moment
I saw this didn't matter.
That was four lifetimes ago...

The day before yesterday,
driving home in my *Astra*,

I happened to look up
at the sky to see
that same cold sun,
even though it was June,
and not January, and
another century, entirely,
and I was astounded at
how these two moments
were joined together
and always had been.

06.23.01

L'hôtel de ville 03.15.59

We stopped at the
Bazaar de l'Hôtel de Ville
to pick up skewers
for a Sunday barbecue.
Flags fluttered over the City Hall.
Awnings around the store
were swollen with the wind.

Cheap clothes spilled
into afternoon shadows.
A salesman, demonstrating
the latest gadget
for slicing a cucumber,
winked at a woman sealing
documents in plastic.

Crowds swarmed out of
side street cafés and
on to the open square.

You were 21 and drinking
more than your fill.
It was unforgiving spring.

People seemed content
- but not for long.
Cruel luxury was just
around the corner:
(the long-anticipated Sixties).

I lost myself in the moment,
for a moment,
perceiving everything happening
at one and the same instant in time.

You drained the last mouthful
of beer from my glass, *again*.
A glutton for pleasure,
you didn't feel you'd gotten it
until you'd stolen someone else's.

Printer's ink 05.05.59

I sat down next to an old soldier
in a hideously remodelled seaside café
on the outskirts of Carnac,
on the south coast of Brittany.
He seemed on the verge of tears
for reasons I couldn't even guess at.

Before long, he got to talking
about his first posting
in the French army,
near the town of Châteauroux.
It was boring stuff,
though soon becoming bloodthirsty,
(Algeria segueing into Indochina),
and I found myself
listening to him intently:
The Americans thought they could do
in Vietnam what we couldn't do!

I asked him when he joined the army.
He told me it was in Forty-Nine:
exactly ten years before
I worked in Châteauroux
peddling Colliers Encyclopedia
to the American airmen billeted there...

Once, when my then girlfriend, Monika,
went to visit her mother in Germany,
I was left in charge of our black poodle.
The dog was a magnet for the ladies

wherever we went - particularly
when I was sitting in a café terrace.

As soon as I sat down in one,
near the Odeon, a young oriental
woman stopped to play with her.
She told me she was half Vietnamese,
with a French army father.
I soon realized I was being picked-up.
Ly had a melancholy quality about her.
She was one of those Parisian students
who lived from hand-to-mouth
and who moved from room to room.
She was enrolled in the School
of Oriental Studies at the Sorbonne,
and was keen to trace her Vietnamese roots.

We went back to my rented house in Gagny,
where she crouched down in the car
when we drove into the driveway
to avoid my nosey neighbors.
I noticed scars on the inside of her arms
when Ly undressed that night.
She confessed she'd done this to herself.
(A *cutter* in the cold terminology
of today's social worker or psychotherapist.)
She said she didn't know why she did it;
but this put me on my guard, and probably
made me keep her at a distance.

She accepted my girlfriend,
though she seemed disappointed,

when we discovered
there wasn’t a lot of fire between us
- nor was there much affection.
(I suppose neither of us had been
expecting a great deal of either.)

Over the next few days, in Châteauroux,
she walked the dog while I flogged
my books to the American military.
We'd retire to our hotel room
after a copious evening meal:
I with the Herald Tribune (Paris Edition),
and she with a textbook on Southeast Asia.

Ly insisted I wash my hands
before she let me touch her
with my ink-tainted fingers,
as I'd been reading a newspaper.
(This detail remains a highlight
of our week together.)
We went back to Paris at the end of the week
and never saw each other again.

A year or so later, I met an engaging
American student who was planning to cycle
from Paris to the Côte Azur and back again.
(Actually, he hopped on a train with
his bike before he was halfway there.)
He told me he was having an affair
with a self-destructive
French-Vietnamese woman called Ly.

He was taken with her,
but found her hell to live with.
What did I think he should do?
I said I didn't know what to advise,
and I had the good sense not
to mention that week in Châteauroux.

Pateras 10.08.59

I found my mother
in that small dark-green
apartment in Manhattan,
where I had spent weekends
and summer breaks before
I left for Europe.
Almost two years later,
I received the telegram:
her husband, my father, was dead.
Leaving you behind, in Paris,
I flew home for the funeral.
My feelings for him being so
mixed, (as they still are),
the trip represented little more
than a week's holiday in New York.

I was surprised my mother
had made so many new friends
among the neighbours
- people I'd never met.
After the funeral,
she offered them cold cuts
from the corner delicatessen.
These acquaintances seemed
closer to her than I was.
Their gestures of condolence
reflected her own warmth.
I remember a young
black woman holding her
through the dream-like wake.

I was the outsider,
only passing through;
a little ashamed of the furniture;
a bystander from a previous world.

I was glad I'd avoided seeing
my father's body lying in state.
The burial in a vast Westchester
cemetery was suburban and
utterly lacking in character.
It did not connect with anything
I knew about the man.
I imagined the old sailor
might have preferred
to be buried at sea.

The rest of the week segued
into a brief adventure.
I went up to Academe,
got lucky with the Europhile friend
of my ex-wife's old roommate,
who was still at the college...

Three years before,
the roommate had complained
to her hot-headed boyfriend,
that I'd been rude to her
in a sexually provocative way.
(There may have been
a grain of truth in this.)
He confronted me while
I was still in Lileth's,

(my future wife's), bed,
challenging me to get up
and fight like a man.

I managed to calm him down,
after pointing-out I'd been
his girlfriend's counsellor
at summer camp a few
years before, where I
was always joshing with her.
So, my greeting her
with the words, *Hi, sexy*,
was merely playful,
and absolutely innocent.
(No innocent, herself,
she claimed to have been to bed
with a famous Calypso singer.)
The boyfriend bought it,
surprising himself at not
having hit me once...

I took the roommate's friend
to the derelict Old Coach-house,
where I spread-out my Harris
tweed jacket on the bare
floorboards for her to lie on...
We arranged to meet in my
mother's apartment in
New York a few days later,
but after taking one look
at that admittedly shabby place,
she lost interest...and left.

I spent my last days in New York
in a whirlwind, looking-up friends,
buying books and records,
without a thought for my father.
The sales assistant in *Sam Goodies*
asked me where I'd bought
my resplendent Tweed jacket.
I told him I'd had it made-to-measure
in London, from whence it was
forwarded to my address in Paris.
He looked at me as though
he wanted to trade lives.

I left the next day and I didn't
see my mother again for four years,
when I pitched-up on her doorstep
with a wife and child, in tow,
and another on the way.
In the meanwhile, you stood
between me and that wife
- stood-in, rather, as,
of all the qualities that
coloured our days together,
permanence was not one.

Japanese sex 10.14.59

In the taxi from the airport,
it emerged you'd
been seeing my friend, Andreas,
while I was away.
Did he ply you with
anecdotes about his
old boss, Aristotle Onassis?
Were you confessing
to a greater intimacy?
Did you have sex
with him, Monika?
No, you only kissed him,
you said, looking away.
I had my doubts...

That afternoon, we started
to fool around on a bed
beside another couple:
another Greek-American
and *his* German girlfriend.
It wasn't an orgy,
just a moment of communal
snogging that went
further than expected.

After a week apart,
we *wanted* to, but,
in the circumstances,
couldn't really *do* it.
The presence of the others

was the problem,
but this also brought
with it a certain
exhibitionistic charge.
They wouldn't leave,
so we went on
kissing furiously,
while I tortured
your breasts.

We made love, somehow,
without actually moving,
(hardly moving, anyway),
and ultimately toppling
our finely balanced
domino of desire.

Wuppertal 10.30.59

Not without a little
trepidation, you knocked
on the front door
of your parents'
flat in Wuppertal.
Your mother took
an instant dislike to me,
undoubtedly because I was
an American, living
the life of a vagabond,
when I wasn't posing
as a student in Paris
- perhaps she just didn't
like the looks of me.
You introduced me as
your *verlobte*, your fiancé,
(a cover story invented
to lend a veneer of dignity
to our tenuous relationship).

I understood, when
your mother called me
a *zigeuner*, a gypsy,
but I fought an impulse
to walk straight out
of her house, out of
respect for all the gypsies
murdered by the Nazis.
Italian by birth,
she harboured that unique

xenophobic hatred
only a foreigner
can reserve for another.
She was smaller,
more wiry, than you
and had suffered
greatly in her life.

The war had left your
father partly paralysed
and in constant pain.
He was so accustomed
to living in his own
fiendish Hell, that,
when you accidentally
shut the car door
on his fingers, he didn't
cry out, as any normal
person might have.
Instead, he accepted
the agony as part of
his generalised martyrdom.
None of us even noticed
until we saw the silent
anguish on his face.

My pity for him
was alloyed with loathing,
after you recounted
a story he'd told you
about his part in the war.
As an officer in Yugoslavia,

he'd lost all sympathy
for the Serbs when
he came across a group
of German soldiers
murdered by partisans
and left to rot
by the side of the road,
each with his own severed penis
stuffed into his mouth.
He told you how he'd
gone berserk at seeing this,
leaving the form of his
reprisals to your imagination.
I think the moral of the story
is that brutality invites
more of the same.

Your mother served
her tangy Sauerbraten,
marinated for a week,
shaking her head as she
stared at me disapprovingly.
On our last night,
you crept into my sofa bed
in the living room and we
fell into what the English
used to call, *bundling*.
In the morning we went
for a ride on Wuppertal's
famous monorail.
With undisguised pride,
you pointed-out the Bayer factory:

that no-nonsense Schloss
which dominates the town.

We found the Autobahn
and headed for Paris
that same night.
Leaving Wuppertal
had been a great relief.
Losing your parents,
losing Germany,
felt very good.

Babies in limbo 02.12.59

I bought the makings of my one
meal a day from the local *Monoprix*:
spaghetti and a tin of tomato paste.
Brother Charlie once told me I suffered
from an over-privileged childhood.
Perhaps I needed to be poor.
You ate an au pair's dinner with
the French children in your charge,
gagging on the watercress soup
when you fell pregnant.

After the first abortion the Swiss
gynaecologist handed you a diaphragm,
which you promptly scissored to bits
in a fit of pique and guilt.
But you got pregnant again
and we found ourselves back in Zurich.
That same doctor performed the abortion
after we promised not to come back.
To make his point, he tried to show me
the foetus, in a kidney-shaped
stainless-steel bowl, but I refused to look.

Amazingly there was a third time.
As I had no money for Switzerland,
this time, a young Greek/American,
of a philanthropic bent,
offered to help, though I barely knew him.
It was a gratuitous act of grace.
So I sent another child to limbo in Geneva.

(Some would say they're one-and-the-same.)

I was determined to pursue the literary life,
ignoring the truth that poets
must be the most practical of people,
with the possible exception of actors.
But I grew tired of living on air pie and
spaghetti with a few chickpeas thrown in,
(nicked from my French-Algerian flatmate).
It wasn't working, any longer, nor were we.

I got fed-up with the *Monoprix* routine,
so I put the poetry on ice, again,
and went after American money on the
US bases at Orleans and Chateauroux.

Perjury 04.06.60

We had a row driving
through the outskirts of Paris.
You handed me back my ring,
(the way they do in the movies).
I promptly flung it out of the window.
You begged me to stop the car,
to look for it in vain
among tarmacked weeds.
I bought you another, but
the promise lost among the
pis-en-lits was not renewed.

Your mother had a point
in calling me your gypsy fiancé,
I marvelled at how parental
disapproval could have driven
so blunt a wedge between us.
Your father - still fighting
World War Two, fifteen
years after the fact -
said nothing. He didn't have to.

I am surprised at how
these vanishing moments
crowd the present, still.

You went to prison
after perjuring yourself,
(at my behest), before an
unforgiving German court.

We'd spent a week in April
outside Kaiserslautern, where I
was flogging books to the military
of the American Empire.
By day we cleaned and polished
my old V.W. cabriolet
with water from a stream.
I was going to trade it in
for a cherry red Opel
I'd discovered in a used car lot.

The dealer pocketed my deposit,
promising to reserve the car.
But he must have had a better offer,
as it was sold when I returned.
I tried on Charlie's technique
for getting results by creating
uproar and embarrassment,
while venting my indignation,
hoping to hold the dealer to his word.
(It had worked in a Manhattan
camera shop seven years before.)
But this was to be the last time
I pulled it. Three lackeys
came out of the woodwork,
brandishing lengths of two-by-fours,
intent on beating my brains out.
I escaped, to find you waiting in the car,
and we managed our getaway.

I persuaded you to swear
you'd witnessed it all.

But you'd actually *seen* nothing,
and you were contradicted
in court by a procession of
mechanics and office workers,
in their lying Sunday best.
That's how matters stood
when the public prosecutor
dropped by to question you,
when you came home for Christmas.
He teased-out your confession,
effortlessly – your German
schoolgirl conscience
being no match for his guile.
You got six months behind bars.

Yellow 05.04.60

I had the VW cabriolet resprayed
when it began to cough its last.
The mushroom paint was
matched in a laboratory, but
I didn't order enough of the stuff.
So when I handed over the paint
to an old Pole who sprayed cars
in his garage in the Paris suburbs,
he told me he needed to extend it.
His methods being far from scientific,
and, as he had no eye for colour,
the car changed from sober
buff to screaming yellow.

I was horrified, but people noticed the car.
As I was going to auction if off,
being noticed was an advantage.
The Pole gave some bits of visible
undercarriage a lick of black paint.
He likened this to *putting on a tie and socks.*
I mourned its previous incarnation.
The mushroom car, a gypsy caravan
of adventure and romance, whose colour
had been a transitional colour between
the then and now, hit the immoveable
yellow buffers of the present.

I parked it in front of American Express,
with a sign displaying its reserve price.
Fortunately it could still move,

though only *very slowly*.
An old American couple outbid
the others; they drove the car to
a Volkswagen factory in Germany,
and brought it back with a new engine.
I almost wept when I saw the oldies
whizzing along the rue de Seine,
with the top down, one evening...

One year later, I heard you
had gone to prison for perjury.
I had put you up to it: to swearing
you'd seen something you hadn't.
But it *had* actually happened,
though just out of your sight, as you
waited in the still-mushroom VW.

The brightest star 08.08.60

My fist connected with your jaw:
the only time I ever hit a woman
- a girl, as you were barely twenty-one.
When you asked me, *why?*
I said I honestly didn't know.
It could have been the panic
of our impending separation,
or leftover anger from the week before,
when I'd deciphered a debauched entry
from the German encoded in your diary.

It began like this:
Orgy with Hilda and two G.I.'s.
Went on all night...
It spared no lurid details.
You were abashed when I confronted you.
I'd unravelled your enigma.

But the very transience of
what there was between us
was holding us together,
recognition of this impermanent
state of affairs fostering
a sort of liberation.

It happened in the car on
the road back to Paris,
on our last week together.
I bounced cheques for petrol
all the way up from Spain,

and I replaced them all with
postal orders, two years later.
(Don't try this when you next
go there, as writing a rubber cheque
is a hanging offence in France.)

Two weeks before, we'd stocked
up on sausages and cheese
from an American PX.
I converted my '52 Hudson into a
mobile bed, and we drove straight to Pilu,
on the soon to be desecrated Costa Brava.
(Travel books referred to Ibiza as
an *untouched paradise* in those days!)

We ended-up sleeping on the beach
and living on tortillas, twirled by
an old lady in a beachside hut.
You flirted with a handsome café owner,
who seemed to want you badly.
He encouraged me with free drink to sing
forbidden songs of the International Brigade
- this in the middle of Franco's reign.
Perhaps he'd hoped I'd get arrested,
so he could have you to himself.

The brightest star in the Spanish
firmament was *Telstar*, America's
first communications satellite,
symbolising American hegemony.
Truly there were no more Americas,
as Charlie Baudelaire had written

a hundred years before, because
everywhere was *becoming* America.

I swam a long way out one tipsy night
and, when I looked for the harbour lights
to guide me back to the beach,
I saw lights in every direction.
Not being much of a swimmer,
I made for what I *hoped* was the beach,
wondering whether I might be
heading out to sea, instead
- at the time, it didn't seem to matter -
before, by sheer dumb luck,
I fought my way back to shore.

Human elevator 07.07.61

You came to Paris
for a weekend,
after your release.

Over a coffee on the
place St André des Arts,
you told me about
your prison conversion
to Communism - a flirtation
born of bitterness.
The other women called you
der menschliche Aufzug,
the human lift,
because you were
always carrying something
up and down stairs.

Mindful of the film
Mädchen In Uniform,
I was overcome with guilt,
(but not one ugly word from you).
After a silence, you asked,
with typical bluntness,
Will you fuck me, Chris?

In your hotel room,
off the rue de la Harpe,
you allowed me closure.
Nothing overtly sentimental,
just goodbye

with uncomplicated sex.
Offering yourself doggy-fashion,
(which you hadn't done before),
you turned me into
a stranger, at a stroke.

In that over-heated
overly beige hotel room,
(and hoping I'd be proved wrong),
I had a premonition
your life would be tragic.

Volume I *Saturday night girl* is the first part of an epic poem, entitled, *You are there forever…*, by Christopher Kypreos, which is to be published in four volumes. Volume I is presently available. The other three, which will appear shortly, are:	£7.95
Volume II *Jill the bad blonde*	£7.95
Volume III *The Monster with beautiful words*	£7.95
Volume IV *The barbarians and the meter maid*	£7.95

Please allow for postage and packing.
Free UK delivery.
Otherwise, Europe: add £2 per book
The U.S.A and the rest of the world: add £3.50 per book

To order directly from Running Man Editions, please fill in this coupon and send it to:

Running Man Editions
5 Leopold Road
London NW10 9LN
U.K.

Mail Order +44 (0) 20 8965 6779
Email: rmeditions@yahoo.com
www.christopherkypreos.com

☐ I wish to order ____ copies of *Saturday night girl.* I enclose a UK bank cheque made payable to Running Man Editions (or the equivalent in International Reply Coupons) for £_________
☐ Please add me to your mailing list and keep me informed of the publication dates of Volumes II, III and IV.

NAME (BLOCK LETTERS)……………………………………………..
Address……………………………………………………………..
……………………………………………………………………………
……………………………………Postcode……........................
Email………………………………......Telephone………………
Signature……………………………………………………………